Schools of Architecture

Bart Goldhoorn (editor)

NAi Publishers

Schools o
Architec

Contents

edited by Bart Goldhoorn

with contributions by

John Hejduk

Stanley Tigerman &

Eva Maddox

Christophe Girot

Arthur Wortmann

Fred Feddes

Competition jurors

Wim van den Bergh

Juhani Pallasmaa

Elia Zenghelis

Preface

Ton Idsinga

Deputy director of the Netherlands
Architecture Institute

Good education forms the basis of the quality of future designers. The nature of this education, the manner in which knowledge and skills are imparted and understanding of the discipline acquired, is decisive for the quality of our built environment. It was for this reason that the Netherlands Architecture Institute decided to draw attention to the education of architects, urban designers and landscape architects with a series of activities during the 1995/96 academic year.

The activities included a series of lectures, seminars and exhibitions examining the theory, practice, history and future of the architectural discipline within and beyond the institutes of learning. Furthermore, the programme included an international student competition with entitled 'The School of Architecture as a Subject for Design'.

Two books have resulted from these activities. One, a Dutch language publication, focuses on the history and current state of the architectural discipline in the Dutch context and the consequences for architectural education in the Netherlands. This English language publication addresses international developments in the field of architectural education via the results of a student design competition and the texts of lectures given by three well-known educators.

The present book offers you an interesting insight into the current thoughts, aspirations and ambitions of students and teachers of architecture.

Lectures

A lecture series was organised by the NAi in the autumn of 1995, together with the Academy of Architecture in Amsterdam. It included renowned educators such as **Raoul Bunschoten, John Hejduk, Dan Hoffman, Christophe Girot, Daniel Libeskind, Stanley Tigerman and Eva Maddox.**

Unfortunately space did not permit us to publish all six lectures and it was necessary to make a selection. Of course John Hejduk, one of the godfathers of architectural education could not be left out. His impressive tale of his life and work at the Irwin S. Chanin School of Architecture at the Cooper Union in New York shows clearly why he is a source of inspiration for many young educators. Hejduk seems to have followed his own fascinations all his life, leading his students through the intriguing secret world of form and objects. That this world is more or less detached from everyday professional practice outside Cooper Union's building is not his main concern.

Although he may have fewer followers then Hejduk, Stanley Tigerman has also been involved in architectural education all his life. Always looking for new challenges, he recently, together with Eva Maddox, founded Archeworks, a cross between an architect's studio, designer's workshop and traditional school. He sees this school as an alternative to traditional professional practice and to regular architectural education, both of which in his view lack a connection with the real needs of society.

The third lecture, by Christophe Girot, chairman of the landscape design department of the Ecole Nationale de Paysage in Versailles, takes a clearly European approach. The permanent questioning of the subject of design that is so evident in American contributions is absent here. In the European context the position of the architect is not (yet) marginalized to the extent that it is in the USA; the architect still seems to have a more or less organic place in society. Furthermore, education is a public institution and much more separate from the private practice of the educator. Maybe this is the reason why Girot's lecture does not focus on his own or his students' explorations, but on the question of education as such: how should one educate the professionals who will be responsible for shaping our future landscapes?

John Hejduk

I seldom have been asked to give a lecture on education. I have taught over 43 years! I said to myself: 'I don't want to talk about education because I have been teaching for so many years.' But then I changed my mind, because, I said: 'Well, what is eduction? And how can I possibly talk about education?' I realised that I also had to partially shape a biography and autobiography. One is supposed to be very proper and talk objectively and separate oneself -the subject from the object- and I was unable to do that. I also couldn't speak for the school that I've been associated with for thirty years because so many other people were involved in the education process

at Cooper Union and contributed in an incredible, valuable way. So, all one can do as an educator/architect, is to celebrate the discipline and the figures, architects, and others who were involved in that educational process. It was a process. I wouldn't speak for the others, everybody has different views of what places are about, I wouldn't be an interpreter for my teaching colleagues. All I can speak about tonight is what I know and what I have been involved with as an architect and educator. And I was and am deeply involved with a place, named Cooper Union (fig. 1), which gave an incredible education to me and to my wife.

In 1949 as a student at The Cooper Union I had a landscape architect teacher named Brian Lynch, a delightful Irishman. He taught me a good lesson. He had the habit of putting books on your desk and saying: 'Read this book.' That's a method I've used as a teacher all these years. If a book interests me, I put it on the student's desk and I say, go read it! That book was titled 'Plastic Art and Pure Plastic Art' by Mandarin. I was only 18. And there's that teacher who just put that Mandarin book on the table and said 'You read it.' I don't think I really got into it then, I got into it in my late 20s, and then it had such a powerful impact upon my thought. If you think you'll be an architect, the book is about architectural thought, as well as painting and philosophy.

I recently looked up in a dictionary the meaning of the words to educate. 'To educate is to bring up young persons' - I don't know why they say young persons only - I think old persons should be brought up educated too - 'to give intellectual and moral training, systematic instruction, development of character and mental power.' Then: 'schooling is to train oneself, to bring out, to develop some latent or potential existence.' And the last line, most interesting to me, is to 'disengage your substance from a compound and to infer principle.'

When I entered kindergarten (some sixty years ago) I was given a magical task to create. The art teacher was a woman and I can only remember or see her today as a moving grey silhouette. Yet I sense her being kind. I imagine that the wonderful relationship of student and teacher formed at that moment. That experience has remained with me throughout my creative life. For some reason in the early 1930s women were the art teachers in America. And in fact, were the music teachers too.

Why my memory of that time is so vivid is because of the work she asked us to make. And I suspect the fabrication of the work led me eventually to two life-sustaining disciplines, that is to architecture and to teaching.

That long-ago teacher (now I remember she had long black hair) asked us to bring in a glass pickle jar; we dutifully did so (with our mothers help). The teacher then asked the children to cover the jar with paper mache and let it dry. The next day she gave each student a jar of blue paint and a paint brush. The paint was enamel paint. We knew we were participating in a class community project and we were happy about that.

We painted the paper mache pickle jars entirely blue. That blue has become part of my genetic coding. Yet the best was to come. We let the blue enamel paint dry. Then our long black-haired beauty gave us a jar of yellow enamel paint and suggested that we paint the rim of the jar and we did. And behold! the yellow paint dripped down in rivulets over the undercoat of blue. I will never forget the tactile joy of seeing that blue and yellow relationship.

When all was finished the teacher praised us for the good job we had accomplished, her good words made us feel good . . . yet, still one more thing had to be done. She said we now could put our brushes and pencils in the jar - and we knew about the practical use of works also.

Our kindergarten teacher was a passionate teacher and instilled in us the idea that individual creativity within a willing community of students is a profound social act. Of course at the end of the year of school we brought our jars home and we gave them to our mothers as a gift of love.

The following are some lines from the book Poetics of Music by Igor Stravinsky:

'To explain - or, in French, to explicate, from the Latin explicare, to un-fold, to develop - is to describe something, to discover its genesis, to note the relationship of things to each other, to see, to throw light upon them. To explain myself to you is also to explain myself to myself...'

To be within the Great Hall (fig. 2) of The Cooper Union for the Advancement of Science and Art is to be within a spiritual place. An institution that is lovingly held in trust. A place that believes one of society's prime social responsibilities is towards learning and education. Learning and education in the deepest sense.

In The Cooper Union's Great Hall

2

Abraham Lincoln delivered his 'Right Makes Might' speech when there was Civil War in our country in 1864 - in this place where my wife and I, and others have been educated. He gave a major speech stating that the American States had to hold together. The American Red Cross and the Women's Suffrage Movement had their offices at Cooper Union, and Peter Cooper himself accompanied one of the great suffragettes in America into the building, because everybody was going wild against them outside, and Cooper took the speaker through the crowd and brought her up to the stage on his arm. Cooper Union housed the first public library in New York. This place, The Cooper Union was founded by Peter Cooper, a man with a vision. A vision that still sustains and maintains the spirit of place and cares for enlightenment. A necessity, particularly in our time when chaos runs rampant. And in some, so-called sophisticated circles and other circles chaos is even celebrated. A necessity, particularly in a time when our own very language is being subverted. Sometimes we enter places and buildings and we leave them not knowing their histories, more profoundly, their spirit. We don't stay long enough. During one event we're already anticipating the next event. We are mobile and free . . . perhaps? I think speed fixes, makes things static. I think to take one's time opens . . . expands . . . makes things flexible.

I remember as a child living in the Bronx one could feel time. The 1930s in the Bronx was old time . . . time to be savoured. Yes, the Bronx, was filled with spirit time. It was presently remote. The trolley cars were the carriages of slow times. Neighbourhoods in the Bronx of the 1930 were older than any neighbourhoods imaginable in Europe. It just felt old. A child knew that it was a place that somehow always had a grey dust sense in the air, even when the sun came out. One understood what the end of the line meant. It meant the farthest distance the trolley car went. It ended in remote areas where the woods began. The woods were sinister places, not for playing. Implied murders were referred to. A trolley line even went out to the water's edge located on City Island . . . City Island held the docks where the ferry departed to Potter's Field, where the prisoners dug the graves of the poor.

One sensed poverty throughout. The Bronx was a frugal place; its atmosphere gave off the air of emptiness and had a profusion of vacant lots. The trolley car was connected to the ground by wheels and to the air by its wires. When moving the passenger felt both connections. He felt the slow, harsh, distant rhythm of the Bronx and he also sensed the reality of ghosts, particularly while waiting in a winter snow storm at night, when

suddenly through the white a single light appeared in the distance and the
warning bell sounded. . . .

Name/place carries weight. . . .The name/place Kafka/Prague carries a
remote darkness. I imagine Munch/Oslo might be another. And surely
Hopper/America. Kafka/Prague - Hopper/ Bronx are not so far away from
each other. The sense of remoteness connects. Kafka's Amerika captured
the tone of the over-overhanging sense of dread. The feeling that something
was wrong and the terror of an undefined situation about to happen. That
is to be in a state of suspended time.

Then I crossed the Harlem river and began my studies at Cooper Union.
And it was there in 1947 in a Humanities class taught by a professor
named Caldiero, who looked like Savanarola, that I was graced by his love
of literature, and read Kafka's Metamorphosis, a singular
architectural event of my life. That is the precise
description of the space of dread or, more specifically, the
space of night and later on I came to know the meaning of
to bear witness and not to forget.

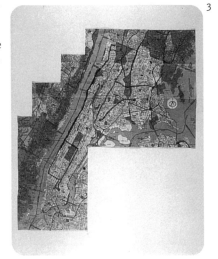

3

One cannot remember the future.

The two places that have provided a sanctuary for my
thought have been the Bronx and The Cooper Union -
places of spirit. And one woman has sustained my soul,
Gloria Fiorentino, my wife and a graduate of The Cooper
Union School of Art.

Look at this map (fig. 3). It shows Manhattan and the Bronx, the places I
happened to live and work in. In the last 32 years there's only one line to
travel from the North Bronx down along the Hudson River, then across town
to The Cooper Union and then back again to the Bronx. It's amazing that
you can live so long and only travel from one place to the other, constantly
going over and over the same route, time and time again. That's been my
travel route basically for 33 years. Not a hell of a long trip but there it is.
These are just a group of slides of The Cooper Union. This is a railroad rail
(fig.4). Peter Cooper rolled the first steel-sections in America, a steel rail,
made for the railroad which had not yet been built. He rolled the rails for
the railroad that was going to go across America. But he stopped then for a

4

while because he was going to build this building, The Cooper Union. And it was one of the first buildings in America that was built out of steel rails. He modified the rail, (the train rail) and it became a structural member inside the building. The foundation footing is solid granite (fig. 5). It is two feet thick by nine feet square. And then 2 inches of iron at the base, and the column is an inch and a quarter- thick cast iron. The building columns were made at that time of cast iron, in 1859.

In 1970 the building had many problems, structural problems, load problems, fire code problems, etc. and it was decided to take most of the building's insides out and put a new building inside, retaining the shell of the old building. In order to hold up the shell, these are the vertical trusses (fig. 6) that were installed and strapped around the building. I had the, I guess you could call it pleasure, and heartache of doing that renovation at that time. I realised in preparing this lecture that the wall shell was free and we were taking something of the old internal organism out, the insides out, of course the outside walls were there, and then putting a new structure in, but the inside wall became the equivocating dialogue between the internal emptiness and the external emptiness of city air and then a new program was inserted in. That's just the very basic scheme of the plan (fig. 7). That's a section through the building (fig. 8). Showing the external walls and this

5

6

7

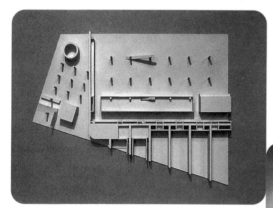

8

new section basically that was put in, and a round shaft for the elevator. At the time elevators were not yet being manufactured in America and Peter Cooper thought that the elevators would be fabricated round. So he built the round masonry shaft, but then when they fabricated elevators in

9 America they were manufactured square. But I want you to see this, there

was a diagonal brace (fig. 9) that moved throughout the building, that held the building, because the building rocked at times. We had to basically lift up floor by floor an eighth of an inch, section by section, each floor in order to install a new steel structure underneath to hold the building up. I'm giving this as a pragmatic lesson. And there is the shaft (fig. 10). That was a 170 foot wall being supported just by whalers (what we call whalers) belts, and the steel truss on the outside. Incredible space actually. This shows what had to be done. There's the original cast iron column, one of them

10

over up there. And the truss, all the new steel had to be set in bay by bay. We jacked up the building an eighth of an inch, section by section in order to get the new structure in. There were friends/ enemies who said: 'Oh, John Hejduk, he's a good teacher and a theorist, but he hasn't built much.' This is a truss that came down throughout the old building (fig. 11) and the contractor chose not to cut it for four days because it was the diagonal bracing for the whole house but the engineer, Professor Peter Bruder, was my professor of structures at Cooper

11

Union in 1949. He said: 'Cut it.' And they cut it. Did you ever see a floating column? That's a suspended column (fig. 12). And that's how it was done. The bottom was cut out because it was actually thick granite walls (100 foot long wall by two foot thick). We had to cut chases and then they took the column and supported it at the top and transferred the load down. By this time the

12

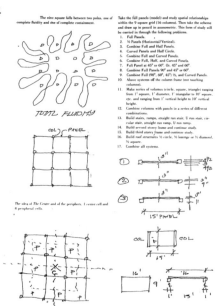

13

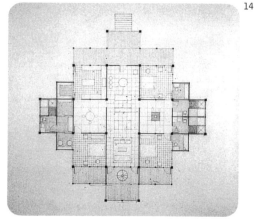

14

new steel was put in and that was lifted an eighth of an inch and then the whole building, section by section was set back down. There were six stories, and we were lifting four. It's about Cooper Union and its pragmatism (we teach four years of Structures).

I want to just go through a series of classic problems that are/were given at the school in architecture. In 1954, I had to study, I felt that I didn't know how to detail. I spent ten years making a set of seven houses, called the Texas Houses in order to understand how to detail and construct. It's as simple as that. More complex a little farther down the line. And this was the original project of the nine-squares (fig. 13), you just see nine squares, there's other things in them, but what interests me about this slide (fig. 14) was that the nine squares were inherent in the first Texas House. The dates were 1953/54, but also the diamond configuration outlines began to be visible. I did seven houses at that time. A very complex study, one just studied for 10 years, about steel, about glass, about walls, about concrete and cement, about stucco, and there were some hundreds of drawings.

What interests me today about architecture being done by architects presently, the simple stuff, I call it modified modern. It's modified modern, there's no intellectual substrata foundation holding the work up, they're beautifully done. I'm speaking of new architecture in Spain, and Holland and other places. Thank God they're simply done. But what's going on in the head is something else again. I wrote about the 'Nine-square' Problem in Education of an Architect, Vol. 1, 1971:

'The nine-square problem is used as a pedagogical tool in the introduction of architecture to new students. Working within a problem the student begins to discover and understand the elements of architecture. Grid, frame, post, beam, panel, centre, periphery, field, edge, line, plane, volume, extension, compression, tension, shear, etc. The student begins to probe the meaning of plan, elevation, section, details. He learns to draw. He begins to comprehend the relationship between two-dimensional drawings, axonometric projections and three-dimensional (model) form. The student studies and draws a scheme in plan and in axonometric, and searches out the three-dimensional implications in the model. An understanding of the elements is revealed - an idea of fabrication emerges.'

Also we are speaking of the nine-square in 1954. It was before Sol Lewitt. The following project was a quintessential ending and that's when I stopped teaching the problem. Lorna McNeur, a woman student who now teaches architecture at Cambridge University in England, made the quintessential nine square kit (fig. 15). That ended the nine-square problem at least from me.

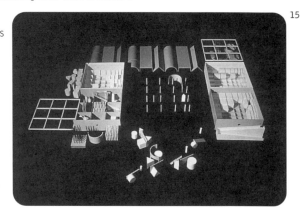

15

People ask: 'What do you do at Cooper Union?' We make things well and we like to fabricate and we like parts. One student in third year did this project (fig. 16). He

16

made all the parts up in our shop. He made all kinds of machines. He found some wheels, I think from bicycles, things like that, and then again the idea of fabrication, of parts, of pieces and then putting them together. He would ride around the school in his invention, but it only went forward, it never went back. His name was Peter Saitta. The next problem given was the 'Analysis' problem where we cut and dissected. We were autopsying buildings, historical buildings of Andrea Palladio and of modern architecture. The strange part of it is, Frank Lloyd Wright's building never came back together again. That was very odd. All the other works we put right back together again, but you never could put Wright's buildings back together again.

This student did a little paper cut-out model of Chartres (fig. 17). Next problem we went to was 'Musical Instruments'

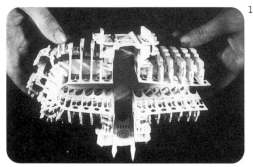

17

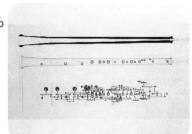

18

(fig. 18). We drew them first: selected a musical instrument, made a drawing of it, sectioning it and then the student made the tools in the shop, and then would make the musical instrument. Again it's the idea of fabrication. And that's what he made. He made the tools and then made the musical instrument with the tools. He made another project that was related to medicine. This young lady's brother-in-law and sister were dentists. This was her Thesis project

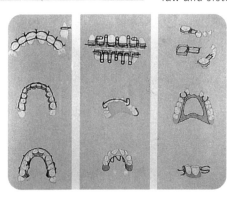

19

20

(fig. 19). It has something to do with dental work. Another one is of literature. I made that list in 1969 (fig. 20). I was a reader of Gide and Proust and all the French authors and I think French literature has had a tremendous impact on architecture. I made this list of what I thought Gide's situation was, and what I thought

Sparse

Precision of organi
Precision of structu
Pruned form
Planar - 2 dimensio
Linear
Reduction
Subtraction
Clarity
Sharpness
Shortness
Tension
Ambiguity
Contractions
Frontality
Expansiveness
Straight - Direct

GIDE

Proust's situation was - but what interests me is that Gide in 90 pages in one of his novels, Wide as the Gate, or - Straight as the Gate, thank you Gloria - is 90 pages, it is absolutely opaque, there's an opacity in that work, whereas Proust, when he remembers things past, is packed dense, full, thick, and then becomes clear.

I found out that Proust had another way of working and what Proust did is he kept on filling and elaborating and more filling and more elaboration and it became clear, where Gide was compression and opaque. Proust was filling, thickening and clarifying.

21

The next area we went into was painting. And I take this painting only for this reason, Uccello had a big impact on my life (fig. 21). Particularly the three paintings, The Battle of San Romano. We talk about constructivism, it's all in there. Its all there in Uccello. One student took the spaceman, the first moonman floating out of the space-ship and look: This is the first spaceman floating into space by Uccello, it's quite incredible (fig. 22). It's all debris, they throw the debris into space. They

22

let it float out. And the Uccello Spaceman and present day space objects float out with all the debris and finally it will be so solid in the skies that nobody will be able to move. That's important to understand.

And now the paintings that have influenced me, the painters have been Ingres, Hopper, and Vermeer. I just want to show three; Ingres, Hopper and Vermeer women. The first one is Madame d'Haussonville by Ingres (fig. 23). I won't get into details but this is a very strange painting because the mirror is not a mirror, could be a mirror? not necessarily a mirror. It's not a duplication of her back and her arm is not her arm, it's some other person's arm coming around her.

23

It's monstrous. And this is an Edward Hopper painting (fig. 24) of the theatre, and each of these women are leaning on their chin, their elbow. Next painting, the Vermeer one (fig. 25). So, three different periods and three different painters somehow painting women in a state of suspension, in suspended thought. They're suspended, you can't get

24

25

inside them, in all three cases. And look, Cooper Union. And here's a studio with a naked model (fig. 26) and I love looking at this shot because there she is and she's suspended somewhere else. I mean she's in that space, and she has observers looking at her, the students painting her and she's naked but she's entirely in her own self. Nobody can penetrate that inner space, hers, and I find that very beautiful. This is a Manet (fig. 27). The same thing, again. And then that's important to me as an architect, the idea of a state of suspension, the idea of the suspended column, the idea of

26

27

impenetrability, the idea of privacy, all those things. It's called Picnic in the Park. You have to retrace back again to the Mondrian. Again I did study, years ago in the late sixties and made these important diagrams (fig. 28). If you take a square and you make an isometric of that it becomes that and then if you build up floor on floor it becomes that (fig. 28a). But if you take a diamond and you make an isometric of it, it becomes a square and you build up that way, so it's a flattening out, so while there is a three-dimensional condition of the diamond, of the square into isometric into this condition and then the diamond into isometric which comes as... this is a seminal work (fig. 28b). It's about the collapse of space and the flattening-out of space. And then if you took that, and I have to be a little academic now, if you took that diamond and you began to pull down here, like a string on a kite, you began to stretch it out and thin it out, spatially it turns in. It becomes a line. So that's the sectional condition of the previous work and it's actually like the black hole of Einstein, you just move in, and that's where the line became important to me and the diamond configuration became important because if you cut a diameter line you get a singular line across here and that's what developed ultimately into the Wall Houses (fig. 28c).

This is a drawing Danny Libeskind made when he was a student at Cooper Union (fig. 29). He graduated in 1970. We gave a Cubist problem. This was Danny's work, actually from a class combined with Bob Slutzky who is a painter and taught at Cooper Union, who was doing collages in his class where they were cutting up Mies and Le Corbusier buildings. Danny came up with these drawings and again it's the flattening of the isometric and the flattening-out of space and about the great paper of Slutzky and Rowe, Transparency. This is the Cubist problem I gave. Going into the project stated:

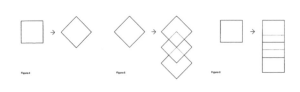

28a

28b

28c

29

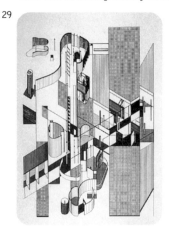

'Do a building in the style of Juan Gris.'

'The "Juan Gris" problem simply states as in that quote - no more - no less. A project evolves or it does not evolve. The problem as given has provoked strong reactions, pro and con, within the student body and faculty. There are articulate arguments against giving such a problem. There are deep reservations about using "Juan Gris" in such a manner. The problem is perhaps one of the most difficult ones to present. Most students reject it outright - some become interested in its implications. A few, using it as a foundation for movement, produce a work. For those who do choose this problem a very thorough analysis into the generating ideas within the paintings of Juan Gris and within the work of the Cubists - Picasso, Braque, and Leger - is made. Relationships between the ideas and work of architects and painters are discovered. An understanding of the organic links is revealed. The pursuit is more than just an historical analysis - for the student produces a work. One finds that the initial statement of the problem launches them into the work of re-creation and finally creation. This, of course, could be the illusionary view of the teacher - the student's reality may be elsewhere. The above does depend on the belief that "Juan Gris" is important to architects and to the issues of today.'

30

Slutzky objected to the 'Juan Gris' problem but I did it anyway. We're talking about the years 1970/1975. Perversions of the above work/ thought in architecture (as we all know) in the last 15 years have occurred by other well know architects. This is a student cut paper project (fig. 30). The interpretation of a Gris painting. I show this slide because of the idea of solidities. It's a marble. Is it marble?

I wrote recently on Adolf Loos's work (fig. 31):

'The first time I entered the imagination of Adolf Loos while I was looking at a photograph. A still photo of an interior that Loos created. If I remember

right it was a room filled with marble walls, pilasters and columns, The overall effect on me was that through the photo I had entered the inner thought of Loos. The veins within the marble were like a multitude of lightning flashes in a

31

dark sky. A sky filled with electrical veins. I thought to myself that I was witnessing the synapses of an architect's brain, captured by an x-ray photo which revealed the workings of a tumultuous imagination. Here was an interior shot of the initial forming of what was to become solid space.'

I want to emphasise that: solid space.

'The surface of the electrifying photo was transferred to the surface of my eyes, then to the inner space of my enclosed brain. In a split moment the room which contained an architectural soul, through the veins of marble, was offered as a gift.

A three-dimensional room was two-dimensionalised onto a flat surface of the photographic paper, which then penetrated my transparent eyes which act as a veil, then to be printed into the folds of my mind. As a matter of fact into the crevices which in a second could will up the image, will up to thought, will up to solidity of thought. Adolf Loos had shown me, if only a glimpse, the soul of marble. A sacred transference of solid space occurred. I have often thought of the meaning of the interior marbled end papers of a book. Books are the tombs of thought. The marbled veins of the internal end papers are internal veils that have printed on them the three-dimensionality of the outside world. The internal wall lights with a Loos room are sometimes covered with seemingly opaque cloth. Thick veils that hide/mask a mysterious light.

When a book is shut its interior is darkened, perhaps the marbled paper gives the internal pages of the book the illusion of momentary flashes of light through the paper's veins. That is, light is sent through vein lines into the sentences of the book.

A book is the sacred tomb of past thoughts. A house is the implied tomb of voices that have spoken into the house's space. Past happiness and past sadness are commingling, giving off inexplicable qualities/tones. The architect is able to set a total framework, which is inevitably affected by the tones of the inhabitants of the house. Mysterious houses become so by the interweaving of the two (subjects and objects). Loos understood this. Loos made a thick internal space so that thoughts could be retained/caught/solidified until the opaque veils could be lifted, removed, dropped to the floor, exposing the nakedness of an anticipating sensual architecture. An architecture in love. An architecture making love...

The book's covers are the lids of a future sarcophagus, which when opened are filled with thoughts...about persons and places, about life and death, about relationships. When the lids of our eyes open at dawn they open from a dream-filled night to welcome the day...

The book in fact is a volume of solid space where our imaginations can roam. The mass, the cladding, are made of delicious air which surrounds and permeates the book, ever-moving...towards an unknown sound...'

I'd like to add:

'I breathe because it keeps me alive. But there is a more important reason. Because when I breathe the air in I breathe in all the sounds from all the voices since the beginning of time. All the voices that have placed thoughts into the air. That is, thoughts escaping from the soul through the voice into the air which I breathe in. Sounds that I cannot hear. Silent sounds filling the air that generations have spoken into, consequently filling me with

worlds that are an invisible text, an invisible sounding text which mingles my thoughts that are invisible. In essence an internal communion takes place giving the sense of the sublimity of silent trans-ferences.'

33

A recent problem I gave at Cooper Union for the students. They were asked to investigate

32 fruit. I showed them a Cezanne still life painting of fruit (fig. 32), a drawing a student had done of fruit (fig. 33) and a bowl

of artificial fruit (fig. 34). And I had made a similar bowl of actual fruit exactly like the artificial fruit. So when you saw the two bowls of fruit from a distance, you didn't know which was the real and which was the unreal. And then I brought the students in and I said: 'Now, here's the two bowls of fruit and here is a Cezanne

34 painting of fruit. Which do you think tastes the best?' And 95% of the students said, the actual fruit tastes the best. And I knew I had a problem. And I said, let's do a year's work on fruit (fig. 35). Which they did - and we had a

35

36

marvellous, we had a wonderful year. Because what they did is, they brought fruit into The Cooper Union building. And they cut it and they kept it, and they kept it and it dried, and all of a sudden for the first time in 30 years there was a different smell in the building. The whole school was filled with rotting fruit, the idea of rotting fruit, and then after the fruit the fruit-flies came. And then the school was filled with fruit-flies. And after the fruit-flies, mice. The superintendent of the building said: 'We can't take this fruit anymore. There's too many mice.' But it was an incredible year we had, dissecting fruit, seeing how it lived, and died, and dried. It was glorious (fig. 36). And the students began to make fruit, to cut fruit, make fruit out of wood. I asked them to make a fruit out of wood that tasted like the fruit. I didn't think it could be done but they did it. And then one young lady at the end designed a house which her husband said he promised to build, and he will build this house for her (fig. 37). That's an ink blot (fig. 38). I did an ink blot and I blot my pear, a pear out of an ink blot. This is from a student who comes from Pittsburgh, a steel family. For generations they were steel workers. And that, ladies and gentlemen is a pear, an orange and a banana that he had just taken out of the furnace (fig. 39). And these are the grapes on the head of Bacchus (fig. 40) and I always say I studied this sculpture of Michelangelo for years and years and the piece I read on the breath convinced me that breath is coming out of his mouth. How do you do that? I just want to know that as an archi-

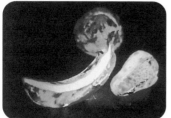

38

37

tect, how can you do it? How can you make a piece of marble and you actually feel the breath coming out of this mouth? That's a real architectural task, about space, about air, about solidities.

NB. Figures 1, 2 and 31: copyright Roberto Schezen

39

40

Some Thoughts about Landscape Education at Versailles

There exist three distinct ingredients which contribute simultaneously to landscape design education. The first ingredient is the person i.e. the student which I will name the 'self'. This person comes into our school with an existence and a destiny or his or her own, a particular family background with beliefs and taboos. The student is a vessel. This vessel receives and transforms pedagogic ingredients. Success in design education depends not only on the importance of family, but also on each student's intuition, emotion and sexuality. The 'self' is very much like a sphinx; it is quite difficult to assess the impact of one's teaching on a student. It is often a matter of time, reason and persuasion, at other times and in other cases it is more a matter of passion and seduction that brings the message across.

The second ingredient is the particular pedagogic method which a school promotes. I would divide landscape teaching along two lines. The first one bases education on a system of certainty, the second on a system of doubt. The first teaches landscape fundamentals with analytical and deductive methods that give clear, multi-layered readings of the environment. This methodology has many advantages when one needs to analyse complex environmental situations. It allows students to distinguish essential points and to accumulate important data about a specific place and situation. Then comes the step that I would call deductive design, where the sum total of the analytical layering is supposed to yield a positive project. This is where the system of scientific certainty shows its weakness, for it assumes on the one hand that analytical information is a good functional way to apprehend the world, and it assumes on the other hand that a young student can imagine a good design from a choice of analytical deductions. This is simply not true. Design education is a slow and imperfect process, it requires years of trial and error before even reaching the semblance of a goal. How on earth can design be considered as innate to a student? Analysis feeds immediate certainty in the mind of student, through a supposedly fool-proof scientific method. The sense of risk and doubt is eliminated, these in turn induce invention which is the basis of design education.
This is why I opt unashamedly for the second pedagogic method which is

based on systematic doubt and uncertainty in design education. I know that it is rather difficult to defend such a position, but I would argue that it is most important for young designers to understand themselves and their outlook on life and the world at large, before hiding behind a fool-proof method of design based on analytical deduction. Design Is about trial and error, about questioning and receiving. Of course, I think that analysis has its place in design, but only once the design intuition is sufficiently grounded and developed to nurture a dialogue between concept and information. It is most important to train our students to open their minds and think for themselves, rather than to push them to conform to a single scientific methodology. The landscape at large is far too complex geographically, historically and culturally to assume that an initial analytical grid is enough to inform and inspire a project. I have often been marked emotionally by a place that I discovered naively for the first time. All the sensitivity and intuition derived from such moments is not quantifiable, yet I firmly believe that these feelings serve as the basis of good design.

The third ingredient is the spatial and material world around us that the Greeks referred to as 'phusis'. It informs us about day and night, hot or cold, wet and dry, windy or calm etc. The world refers to our senses. The openness or closeness of particular place, the amount of sky or cover, can affect emotions and perception in different ways. This is not to be confused with the internal mood of each person which depends on their way of life. The world at large can be looked at objectively through a phenomenal grid, it is quiet or calm, natural or urban, flat or sloped. All these factors inform and feed a particular design project. They are so numerous that it is up to each person to choose what is really significant to them. Is for instance, the memory of a given place more important than its present form? It depends on a variety of criteria, and we inevitably return to the fundamental question of choice in each design.

Self, method and world come together in a school, and the challenge for the teacher is to take position in his teaching with respect to these three fundamental ingredients. In teaching design, there is a high level of emotional charge and psychology to account for. Some teachers even say that their job is 90 % psychology and 10 % content! This may be a little exaggerated, but psychology and mutual respect are certainly primordial in teaching. As far as ideology and 'isms' go, I choose not to take issue today. For me, learning design is more a matter of individual discovery than one of dogma, to each student his or her own way, at his or her own pace. There are to this day no recipes for landscape education. I believe that landscape design education can only be based on empirical teaching. A good example of such empirical teaching is an exercise that professor Anthony Dubovsky taught me when I was his assistant at U.C. Berkeley. This exercise is rather elliptical but it illustrates quite well the long-term objectives of design pedagogy which are: initiative, autonomy and adaptation to change. He would give a tourist map of the colonial town of Savannah, Georgia to each student with a guide to the old grid town. Dubovsky asked students to shift the entire grid of the town one street over. This meant that instead of stopping according to the guide at the no. 27 of such a street to see the house of some famous gentleman, the students would stop and see what happened at the same number one street over. This is what Dubovsky called a displacement exercise: each student had to tell us what he or she saw, they had to draw and tell us what was of interest at such an unknown address. There was none of the conventional wisdom attached to the place. Everyone had to speak for his or her self. I very much liked this exercise because instead of learning a set of pre-digested information, the student had to discover and react to something in the world that is not described in a book. In this teaching method, there is no preparation, just action. I believe that such an exercise is most pertinent to landscape education today since it is about wit and action in a problem situation.

Either a student expects that a school will help him learn an amount of pre-set parameters. This will result in what I call a cook book approach. Or the student chooses to trust his or her own judgement and act for him- or herself in a variety of situations. The question today is whether landscape education wants to confirm a particular social or environmental dogma, or whether it simply wants to induce reflection in each student without a set of preconceived answers. The former method tends to precondition answers, whereas the latter fosters a genuine kind of intelligence for its time. If we continued to train landscape architects the way we did during the housing boom of the 1950s and 1970s it would of course be wrong and completely displaced. Landscape education must be able to train for the present, but it must also project the student into the future. To this day, I know of no recipe for the future. Each decade has to adapt to very specific situations and changes in morality. Teachers should not act like high priests telling students how to answer and make something. They should create a particular situation and observe how the student reacts and solves the problem. My definition of landscape education is to allow for the intelligence of any given period to materialise inside the school. Pedagogy will always remain the alchemy that yields the spirit of a given time.

There is definitely an emotional charge in landscape design teaching. We are not dealing with an exact science. We teach something that is indefinite and still nascent. There are moments in design education when you want to reassure the student and comfort his or her ideas, but then there is also a time when you need to destabilise a student and push him over the edge of what he or she is willing to accept or understand. In pedagogy, there is both seduction and passion; but there is also deception and disappointment. All this is part of the same process. I would even argue that some students learn more through constructive disagreement, than they would through tacit approval. Disagreement allows for the student to define a position vis-à-vis a teacher. In design education there is always a series of dialectical choices that appear. In Versailles, the learning process does not follow pre-set rules. This brings us back to following the analogy: to learn how to play music, do you need to take prior lessons in theory or do you just sit in front of a piano and start playing ? If we had stuck to the idea that one needs lessons in established knowledge, we would not find blues, jazz and rap in our culture today. These new musical cultures did not come from books, they were invented in the particular feeling and spirit of a given time. I am using this distant analogy to convey the notion of landscape education at Versailles. In design studios, as with painting and drawing, there are moments that are difficult to explain and that remain completely irrational. I would oppose this mode of acting and thinking, to a more established scientific and analytical form of practice. In any situation the student must trust his intuition before even understanding concretely why he or she chooses to do things in a particular way. This mode does not exclude all the knowledge and know-how that the teacher brings. But it is always ultimately up to the student to make his or her own choice. To return to my distant analogy about music, I would say that the piano lesson comes after the sound... first, you play and then you understand what you have been playing. It is just like making love, where you often only understand what happened after it is over. Design is therefore a fundamental part of one's being. It cannot be dissociated from ontological thinking. If a school chooses a pedagogy based on scientific dogmatism individual and intuitive levels are set aside; it becomes a world where landscape is taught in a functional sequence and where a given situation yields a known result.

Our world is changing at a dramatic pace today. It is incoherent and exploded both spatially and socially. As landscape designers, we are asked more and more to adapt to this rapidly changing situation. The pool of existing examples is rather slim. Trends have no place in landscape education. The goal of an educator, in my opinion, is to teach the student how to adapt over time. You cannot calculate or premeditate results in education, the idea is clearly to stay open and informative. Our school has existed for a while, but until this day it has never produced a written program. I'm not sure whether this absence of program is good in the long run, but it shows that landscape education at Versailles has been based on something else which I would call the oral tradition. Each time we ask a teacher like Vexlard or Coulon to send us a written program of their teaching. They answer: 'we don't believe in programs'. So we have no printed trace of their pedagogy; we just know that the teacher comes, brings students together, talks and questions each student's designs. The important thing is what stays imbedded in the student's memory over time.

What would happen if the school started printing what was happening in studios? When in fact the whole education since the beginning at the Versailles school has been based on lore. Some older students who left school a while ago sometimes recall an instant in their education, like a day spent with a particular teacher. This teacher probably said or did something which became really significant to that student five or ten years later. As you can see, there are no prescribed rules in our educational genre, it is primarily a matter of subjective experience and time. I think that teaching landscape architecture is about developing creativity and sensibility in students. Education is about putting a student in a particular situation and understanding how he or she reacts. It doesn't just have to do with an encyclopaedic accumulation of information. Landscape is an incredibly complex mixture of things that are both qualitative and quantitative. We have people arguing in France today that landscape is simply a question of movement through space and fragments. Teaching a theory of chaos as a pedagogic base to landscape architecture would certainly yield catastrophic results. What young designers need is to determine and trust their own way of reaching and making things in the world. I will not name some teachers in our school who are able to do the exact opposite. I have seen some students go into a studio each with their own design personality and come out three months later with the whole group producing identical drawings and designs. In the space of a few weeks, design students can become total clones.

Many younger students ask for that kind of teaching, they want to conform to a style and thus be reassured. Of course, students don't like to be unsure of their work, but it is in this play between stability and instability that design education takes place. There is in my opinion no other way. Students would rather be sure at all times of the work they produce. If they can learn tricks about how to draw and design like their master, then they think of themselves as a piece of the master. But such a token gesture does not guarantee anything in the long run. In my opinion stylistic manipulation leads nowhere in terms of landscape education. A studio on style could be accepted as a one-time exercise in later years, but it cannot be used repeatedly as a dependable teaching method especially in the beginning. I think that the real goal in design education is to capture the intelligence of the moment; it is certainly not to teach students how to regurgitate what someone else has done previously.

There is another problem in landscape design education which is that of representation. We have inherited the perspective drawing system from Alberti, but more often than not this system, which is more adapted to buildings, distorts space and is not applicable to our work. It is really the question of how the world is brought into a project and how far the project goes out into the world. The great Californian landscape architect Thomas Church had no qualms about it. He never drew any plans or perspectives. He simply came to a site with some chalk bags and sticks and drew his design on the ground and staked the site. This had the immense advantage of incorporating the surroundings immediately in the design gesture and it resulted in superb gardens. But this example applies to only very few situations today. We now need to make plans that are legal documents. We also need perspectives to seduce the client and reassure the neighbours. But the use of plan and perspective does not guarantee a good design. We are no longer dealing with immediate space. I'm not so sure whether we teach the art of landscaping to students when we ask them to learn how to draw plans, for they learn a set of conventions that restrict and condense the world in two dimensions. The reality of our profession is far more complex than that, and is probably what keeps us distinct from architects and object designers.

Our work has much more to do with space and time; ten or twenty years is almost nothing in terms of development for a landscape. If we really explained that to any politician they would immediately refuse to work with us. The time factor in landscape architecture is extensive and cannot be fully grasped during 4 or 5 years of education at school. it can only be hinted at. This is also the reason why the profession of landscape architecture is so different from others. It addresses mostly medium-term and long-term goals and for that reason alone it has become ideological and almost subversive in the light of our modern world with its short-term decisions and fast money.

Design education also has to make some fundamental choices. On the one hand, many would be tempted by the idea of landscape as environmental decoration, where students would be trained to work for an immediate result which can be immediately photographed. Landscape design becomes then much more of a graphic and visual exercise. The notion of place and space over time is simply dismissed. Look at the suburban developments of the 1960s outside Paris where the landscape around social housing was planted with fast growing poplar trees. Now thirty years later these mature trees have reached their time and are falling on buildings and people. Everything has to be removed at great cost.

Had they originally planted some oaks or beech, the trees would still be very young today and they would contribute slowly to the character and identity of a place. The trees would still look great one hundred years from now! I would opt for such a planting philosophy in landscape design and orient students towards a work that mends and settles a place durably. When you plant noble trees that last for centuries, it is much harder to put them down after a while. Thus you give a particular status to a place. The main problem is that if you encourage this approach, which is not the designerly media-oriented way, you train students who will barely earn enough money to eat boiled potatoes for the rest of their lives. The best example of such 'selfless' work is certainly Sorensen's campus at Arhus in Denmark. He just planted acorns and it took fifty years for the oaks to grow. Now they look as if they had always belonged to the place.

What is the place of action in landscape architecture education? I would like to return here to the origins of the Versailles school, when it was created as a reaction to the massive destruction of World War Two. The role of this school has always been associated with healing, not only environmental healing, but also cultural and social healing. The 'paysagiste' perceives him or herself as a kind of environmental doctor. He is constantly asked to bring coherence to an environment that has become completely incoherent, particularly in the social housing districts of the suburbs. We have work in these suburbs for the next fifty years. The school could have opted early on for an idealist approach based solely on the history and design of gardens but the core of our work is outside this realm, we are always confronted with the question of incoherent environments in transformation. A good example of this is the French Mediterranean coast and more particularly the Cote d'Azur which has been savagely destroyed over the last thirty years. There is a little town to the east of Nice called Cros de Cagnes where I think Jim Jarmush could easily make a movie without a script. The landscape is totally hallucinating with a six-lane highway separating the village from what remains of the beach. You have the sea with its blue horizon, you have a ten-meter strip of pebble beach where people pile up to roast in the sun. People get killed every month trying to reach the beach with an ice cream cone in the hand. If they get there, they find refuge in this absolute blue horizon, but the sound track is really that of six lanes of diesel trucks and sports cars zooming by. I'm not sure that there is an answer to a place like Cros de Cagnes, but it is interesting to note to this day, that there does not exist a single school of landscape architecture around the Mediterranean basin except for Technology University in Haifa. The Mediterranean coast has very specific problems and we are starting to base some of our education in the third and fourth years at Marseilles. We may not solve all the environmental problems from the Costa del Sol in Spain to Izmir in Turkey, but at least we will start asking questions within the local cultural framework.

The goal of landscape education today is not to give ready-made answers, but to open the debate and ask questions towards the making of a more coherent world. I think that there is always a need for balance between 'realistic' work and 'idealistic' work in landscape education. Intuition finds its source in the ideal. As a teacher you don't want to kill young students in their soul by confronting them with huge quantities of hard scientific reality. I am not sure whether it is helpful to confront a student in his first two years with incredibly complex environmental situations. The important thing is to preserve in each student the dialogue between the ideal and the real which validates a design. Otherwise pedagogy remains meaningless and hollow. The real question for a teacher is how and when to make the real and ideal meet.

The only way to confirm or disaffirm a design is for the students to go out and look at the world. This is why we foster several field trips in our curriculum. This year our first year students want on their first field trip to Dunkerque and the abandoned coal mines of Flanders and Artois. This was not a romantic trip, it was cold, grey and windy, but they saw together with Jaques Simon some very interesting things. The problem with landscape architecture is that it is not in the books yet. And therefore, at Versailles, we consider the voyage as the most fundamental text for education. The first exercise students did during that trip was to pile up mud at high as they could in the middle of a forest. I think that there is a relationship in landscape architecture between the self and the material world when the earth gets stuck under each nail. The contact is basic and fundamental. I think that we have invented a good educational tool at Versailles which balances the contemplative and ideal levels with the direct physical contact with the land. This is probably the reason why 'paysagisme' will always remain an eminently sensual profession.

Stanley Tigerman and Eva Maddox

Archeworks
pedagogically speaking

One of the unique differences between Archeworks and conventional design academies lies in our understanding of that crevice that separates ideation and reality, and how we approached that intersection.

Challenging, yet ultimately rewarding, student teams met on a continuing basis with at least 4 project situations that brought them into contact with: a. day care teachers, b.community organisations, c. manufacturers, and d. SRO operating personnel. Pedagogically, those intersections in turn bred other connections sometimes addressed by our first lecture series, sometimes by the intersection of specialists in the fields being researched, both of which in turn illuminated some minor epiphanies, subsequently led to some preliminary conclusions that are just beginning to bear fruit.

These complexly transmissive relationships are dependent on a sort of contract of communication, the expression of thoughts in spoken words, and, in the case of any design practice, audible drawings, modellings and of course products. These acts of 'speaking' can never be passive. The trajectory flows from speaker to listener regardless of outcome and consequence, question or statement. And the expression of an idea exercises a certain will for power, just as the making of architecture, for example, reflects that will, to greater or lesser degrees. There can be no act in space, be it speech or building, that is without intention. This is especially true within the structure of the university, for teacher and student alike, for it is in the classroom that knowledge is both imparted and questioned simultaneously, and this two-way complicity ranges from the excessively scientific to the perversely opinionated.

In the design lab at Archeworks, where project-specific teams work, this 'situation of exchange' is intentionally exacerbated further for many reasons: the design process can be neither formulaic (scientific, objective) nor artistic (expressionistic, subjective) only, but at the very least both. The discourses of design are constantly mediated through the mechanic workings of specific need and current culture; and perhaps as a consequence of these, it is clear that those who currently 'practice' design - professionals, teachers, technicians, theoreticians, historians - indeed, all those dedicated to its craft, are in complete disagreement as to just how and why practice situates itself in society. In other words, design takes its place on the basis of constantly shifting sets of requirements, functions, contexts, desires, needs, lacks, agenda, aspirations, dream, and of course, opinions.

While in the conventional university, it is clearly the design review, or jurying system where these complexities clash, 'criticism' at Archeworks tends to be actively part of production. Interns, clients, facilitators and various outside experts from industry are here positioned to present, to speak, and the lines of authority (and authorship) so prevalent in academia and in practice tend to blur and shift in hopefully constructive ways. But what constitutes criticism? What is allowed within this seemingly infinite transmission, keeping in mind the necessary and inescapable complications mentioned earlier? If criticism is ever to be constructive, then the 'allowance' that is required within the exchange must always attempt to involve the position of the 'other'. The 'positions' of the listener and the speaker and the complicitous association between them required for any true criticism and active learning must be framed in time and in place. That is, limits must be set, the conditions of the exchange (of knowledge, if one is lucky, but at least ideas, experiences) agreed upon and located in an always reversible transmission.

In the case of the SRO project, an active and continuous criticism (with tools in hand) enabled a rather animated dismantling of not only conventional wisdom, but conventional practice as well. Our purpose was to develop alternative approaches to the all too familiar problems inherent to the type - the lack of space, storage, light, ventilation, character, etc. as 'true' in dimension and materiality as it was, the full-scale mock-up acted as a kind of specimen with(in) which interns could operate. At times it functioned as a huge sketchy surface with marks ranging form crude measurements to elegant graffiti, only to be wiped away in favour of corrugated cardboard aggregations of supposed functionality. And these in turn were critiqued and mercilessly erased so as to make room for a 'solution' constituting a more structurally sound, dynamically adaptable and hybridised system of enclosures, programs and surfaces designed to seamlessly traverse the room.

Modest beginnings in these areas are encouraging. Two students began discussions with manufacturers towards realising a particular product that may yet come to fruition for a portable homeless shelter/shopping cart convertible.

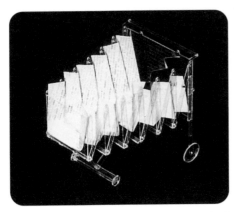

This project recognised and adheres to the major constituents that comprise the mission of Archeworks. First, concentration on the production of a small object. The object seeks to propagate change in a complex system by not engineering a specific centralised outcome, but by adopting a complex adaptive systems approach that will allow a system to evolve and bring about novel results. We fully recognise the necessity to refine the product so far produced. First, simple items of the product will be perfected. Next, new possibilities will be added to the product. We believe there is always the opportunity to make small plans that have far-ranging implications.

For the most part, shopping carts used for their designed purpose can be a frustrating experience. The typical, woeful cart found at the neighbourhood supermarket is a cumbersome beast, prone to almost immediate misalignment. It limps into service and sputters gyroscopically in opposition to its user's desire. Its major shortcoming is the wheels. But carts are versatile and because of their accessibility, they are seized by homeless people. Carts provide a person with a facility to conduct commerce, store personal belongings and give modest sleeping and living accommodation. In a sense, a cart gives the homeless back some of their individuality and dignity.

The Shopping Cart Project, conceived as one solution to the Archeworks program to define the workplace environment of the future, is an attempt to make an object with various configurations that cuts across all social strata to produce change. It is shopping cart, perambulator, travel cart, toy, electrician's wagon, hospital crash cart, dump cart, homeless shelter and through this open-ended flexibility and adaptability levels, warps and inverts the existing social structure. It becomes a formidable tool for the homeless in their war for survival.

Lighter than the standard cart, with an improved wheel disposition, the cart is modular and capable of interconnection with other units, allowing it to be configured in large sheltering systems. It is physically capable of compression and expansion; of folding and unfolding. It is delivered to its commercial environment as a stripped base unit. Once it has escaped to society at large, it can take on useful functions by appropriating objects from its physical context. For instance, the front grate of the cart when unfolded becomes a stove with the addition of fuel. Discarded containers, paint cans and bags can be conveniently affixed to the cart. Discarded building materials such as plywood can be adhered to the cart in order to expand its sheltering capabilities. Plastic trash bags can be draped over and attached to an unfolded cart to offer protection from the rain. Social agencies can provide useful add-ons: portable heaters, headlights, storage modules, and straps are but a few options. We even envision a block and tackle system along with grappling hooks that would allow people to elevate themselves above street level. A series of threaded rods could be expanded between the structural members of an expressway overpass in order to suspend the cart in the ready-made resting crevice. Simple rope ladders could allow people to gain entrance and exit from the nested cart.

The relatively low cost of this cart (approximately $100), affords universal distribution - thus making it difficult to eradicate its use by the homeless. Only when homelessness is adequately and appropriately addressed will the cart as a tool for the homeless disappear.

scaf-fold (n). 1 a temporary wooden or metal framework for supporting workmen and materials during the erecting, repairing or painting of a building, etc. 2 a raised platform on which criminals are executed, as by hanging 3 a temporary wooden stage or platform, as that on which medieval plays were presented 4 any raised framework.

When one sees a scaffold a number of questions are forthcoming. What is the nature of the enterprise within and obscured by the scaffold? Is the 'structure' within being erected, rehabilitated or raised. The scaffold is a temporary structure and as such it is an independent object. It is an enabler, a catalyst if you will for some corresponding change. 'Nature commonly uses interim scaffolding to accomplish many of her achievements.'

Incrementally nature lays one successful accomplishment over another. The opposable thumb was the platform that allowed man to manifest his intelligence through the fabrication of tools. Entire ecosystems can be reclaimed from the brink of extinction if scaffold species are available and not extinct themselves. After a scaffold has been removed we are either left with something new, other or perhaps even nothing.

It is not a far stretch to equate Archeworks with a scaffold, enabler, catalyst and advocate for issues of social, behavioural, historical and ecological concern. Archeworks is the near-extinct species that can allow for repair, renewal and uplift of conditions of deterioration and need. Archeworks is nominally a school of design and as such its first although not exclusive mandate is to bring effect via the practice of the allied design disciplines (architecture; interior, industrial, graphic, environmental design, etc.). Therefore, Archeworks is an interdisciplinary process. Lest

this process be trivialised let a specific mission be outlined:

Archeworks' design methodology seeks to create a demystified language common amongst those participating in the program. Moreover, this mode of expression will be useless if it is not exportable beyond the physical confines of Archeworks. Therefore, Archeworks is committed to a dialogical approach to design that incorporates a rich but commonly intelligible language that enables and includes the publics involved with Archeworks projects to be active participants in the design process. The result sought by Archeworks is an open-ended analysis of the issues being addressed, Thus, Archeworks seeks and encourages open dialogue with a public beyond even the specific projects addressed.

Archeworks recognises society as a dynamic system. Dynamic systems are complex and difficult to quantify. Archeworks' looks incorporate a complex adaptive systems approach to design both in its internal method and externally to the projects and the publics affected. Openness is the goal of such an approach. Such an approach would be characterised by the absence of imposed centralised control, the autonomous nature of those involved, high connectivity between those involved and the networked non-linear causality of peers influencing peers. A complex adaptive systems approach allows a system to evolve, adapt, be resilient, be open-ended and bring about novel results. While the disadvantages are at times frustrating the benefits outweigh the disadvantages. The complex adaptive systems consider the non-linear component inherent in life. 'The network is slippery, ensnaring the unwary in its paradox of no beginning, no end, no centre. Or, all beginning, all end, pure centre. It is related to the Knot. Buried in its apparent disorder is a winding truth. Unravelling it requires heroism'.

Archeworks will seek to apply known strategies that are coherent with the above described systems approach. One such approach is a model for distributed control first used at MIT for the development of small robots:

1. Do simple things first.
2. Learn to do them flawlessly.
3. Add new layers of activity over the results of the simple tasks.
4. Don't change the simple things.
5. Make the new layer work as flawlessly as the simple.
6. Repeat, ad infinitum.

This overlaying of effective responses is one model to deal with complexity. Simple local control will result in distributed control. Simple local control implies a bottom-up strategy that results in complex outcomes. Some of the lessons to be derived from the above approach such as incremental construction were arrived at intuitively by the interns during he first Archeworks session.

The notion of an activist concept of approach to social theory has often revolved around what comes first, theory or practice. What often results from this discussion is a circular dynamic. Archeworks, while not deriding the intellectual necessity of considering the implications of this conversation, opts for theory and practice being of equal import. To this end Archeworks, in keeping with an open-ended discussion of design, opts for praxis which equals reflection + action.

Our general rejection of tenure, prerequisites and accreditation, i.e., those vestiges that define (and in our collective wisdom) delimit conventional design education, is unswerving in its dedication. We remain confident that Archeworks represents a viable

alternative to both educational, as well as practical, traditions in our several design fields, and we remain firmly convinced that with the changing times, combined with the need to operate in a post-disciplinary setting, our collective effort directed toward areas not normally the recipient of quality design work is sorely needed even as it is adventuresome. We do not at all mean to imply that ours is the ONLY way to challenge the several design communities to intersect with areas of real need; the fact is that both Eva and I continue to encourage other organisations in other locations to emerge to do just that. We also do not suggest that Archeworks (or others, for that matter) work far afield from their home communities, since building credibility with sponsors is a full-

time job and should not be taken lightly.

We do continue to believe that there is a place in our society for organisations to emerge that will attempt to redress in small ways inequities where designers, as well as others, need to stand up and be counted (upon). We still believe in our motto not to make big plans but to make each small plan as good as it can be, so that in aggregate, all of these small plans can impact upon society in such a way that each can be brought to fruition.

In other words, and in a genuinely affirmative spirit, we are frankly thrilled that we survived the first year, and that Archeworks seems to grow stronger precisely because of its fluidity. Ours is not a rigid, linear, static operation, but one that engages in simultaneity, multi-dimensionality, and in all events dares to go where angels fear to tread.

Thus is the state of the art of Archeworks at the graduation of our first class of interns. We are encouraged by our growing support systems even as we tighten our grasp of who we are. But make no mistake: we do know for whom we toil.

The students' competition 'The School of Architecture as a Subject of Design' was launched in October 1995, when the competition brief, in the form of a poster, was sent to 826 schools of architecture all over the world. The text of the brief was conceived by Wim van den Bergh, president of the jury, whose other members where Juhani Pallasmaa and Elia Zenghelis.

The aim of the competition was threefold. By offering institutes the possibility of integrating the competition into their course programme, the competition would form an instructive exercise in conceptual thinking and its translation into developed design proposals. Secondly by introducing the theme to students, it would challenge those being educated to reflect on their own situation. And finally, the results of the competition would reveal the ambitions and expectations of a new generation of architects-in-the-making who would be responsible for shaping the environment in the coming decades.

The reactions, as can be seen in the following pages, were overwhelming. After the jury report and a look at the winning entry and the eight honourable mentions, Arthur Wortmann, an editor of ARCHIS magazine, analyses the entries as a whole and discovers ten categories, each representing a distinct approach to the competition brief. This is followed by a quantitative analysis of the entries by journalist Fred Feddes. The book concludes with a list of entries grouped by country and school and ranked according to the number of entries.

Competition Brief

Architecture and Education

Architecture is a profession, the practice of a technical and artistic craft, but it is also an academic discipline. Architectural training occupies the field of tension between these two views. Knowledge and skills can be taught and learnt, but understanding and insight largely have to be acquired by students themselves. Schools of architecture must do justice to all these aspects, creating the time and space for discovering the essence of architecture.

In Perspective

Architectural training has changed considerably through the centuries. Initially, knowledge was imparted in a pragmatic master–pupil relationship, later at educational institutions such as the Ecole des Beaux Arts and the Ecole Polytechnique, and today mainly at large-scale universities and small private establishments. Current technological and socio-economic changes are putting pressure on the architect's position. This will have inevitable consequences for architectural training and the role of educational establishments in that field.

Assignment

What are the future roles of architecture and the architect? Tomorrow's architects are receiving training today. What do current developments have in store for architectural education and the various types of educational institutions? Design a school of architecture for the future and represent it three-dimensionally, basing your conception on your personal vision of the future roles of architecture and the architect.

A total of 424 submissions from students had been received by the competition office by the closing date on April 15, 1996. The projects were viewed, discussed and judged by an international jury during a three-day meeting in Rotterdam in May 1996:

Wim van den Bergh (chairman): Heerlen, The Netherlands
Juhani Pallasmaa: Helsinki, Finland
Elia Zenghelis: Athens, Greece

Secretaries to the jury were Jan Peter Wingerder and Billy Nolan.

All entries were considered by the jury, including those that did not conform to competition regulations. All entries were anonymous, their identification being a six-figure code chosen by the entrants. In keeping with the character of the competition, no selection criteria had been formulated beforehand. Criteria were adopted by the jury during the meeting, based upon the quality of the entries.

The procedure began with a meticulous, time-consuming survey of all entries by each jury member. The majority of projects consisted of two A2 panels and a written statement of 500 words. Each jury member made an individual selection of those projects considered to be worth further discussion. The total number of projects chosen at this first stage was 21. These distinguished themselves either by their unique quality, or stood out among a number of projects sharing a similar thematic approach. The 21 selected projects were those that combined an original concept or observation with a clear translation into a design matching the complexity of the initial idea.

The projects selected in the first stage were:
160196, 171717, 357544, 954184, 9nueve, bi-m, djrbkl, fsarup,

g24k31, ground, inform, kaukei, kkkkkk, maredd, mckm96, mus965, noasis, pe96p2, semo96, torens, xxxll

These projects were then closely examined and compared by the jury. During the ensuing discussion only one project was judged to have succeeded in coping with the overwhelming demands of the brief in that it asserted its independence as a counter proposal. The jury discovered certain recurrent tendencies in the remaining submissions. A significant proportion consisted of incomplete, unresolved, yet collectively instructive ideas and responses to issues and problems faced at the receiving end of architectural education. Eight of these, deemed by the jury to be the most representative, were awarded an honourable mention. In so doing the jury was exercising its right, as laid down in the Competition Regulations, to alter the allocation of prize money. The jury decided to award one first prize and eight honourable mentions. The prize winners were as follows:

Winner: 171717

Honourable Mentions: kaukei, xxxll, g24k31, 9nueve, 160196, 954184, torens, mus965

The jury was surprised by the response to the competition. The huge number of entries from literally all around the world, and the incalculable work and energy invested in the more than 400 projects showed the enormous interest among students in the subject of architectural education.

It is tempting to speculate on the reasons for this huge response. One might find the answer by considering the changing role of architecture in present-day society, both as a discipline and as a profession, or by studying the projects in relation to the educational environment from which they originate. The jury's sole task, however, was to judge the quality of the entries.

In contrast to the quantity, and the often seductive presentation techniques, many entries, however, lacked a strong underlying concept and were disappointing in terms of quality. This was undoubtedly due to the complexity of the task set by the competition. To propose ideas for a future school of architecture is not only a difficult challenge for students, but also for experienced educators and architects. In order to conceive such a project, one must successively develop an attitude to culture and technology at large, the role of architecture, and the methods used in architectural education. Since the student is fully involved in the educational process, it is very demanding to ask for a design concept derived from a clear analysis of this same process. It is reminiscent of one of Baron von Münchhausen's tales in which he claimed to have lifted himself and his horse out of the swamp by pulling on his wig.

One jury member, Elia Zenghelis, felt that the requirements of the task proved to be too great, even overwhelming. The entries were highly illustrative of the fact that answers to questions of architectural education will not be provided by students and that, at this moment in history, these questions are in vain. The picture that emerged reinforced the view that, notwithstanding pedagogical idealism, architectural education amounts to being thrown in at the deep end of a pool brimming with unknown and ever-changing perils requiring unspecified skills and ingenuity; only a few cunning and imaginative swimmers will manage to stay afloat.

Taking into account the complexity of the task it was probably not surprising that a majority entries attempted a physical manifestation of the future school. Most of these projects were formalistic exercises in design without any convincing visionary or poetic basis. Most of these entries read 'school' in a rather one-dimensional way as building and not as idea or, to quote Kahn, an 'inspiration' looking for an 'institution' or a 'Form' to inspire a 'Design'. However, it is evident that in our age of rapid change, where there is a widespread sense of uncertainty and lack of visionary perspective, Utopia is rendered impossible and futuristic aspirations quickly turn into shallow science fiction or exercises in graphics.

It was curious that numerous responses took the form of pessimistic, apocalyptic, anti-utopian views of the future. A number of students reintroduced the optimistic technological utopian themes of the 1960s, but lacked the refreshing spirit of their predecessors. They seemed unaware that the concept 'school' derives from the Latin 'schola' and the Greek 'skhole', meaning 'leisure devoted to learning'.

Other recurring tendencies included an engagement with aspects of change in contemporary society and its impact on architectural education: the implications of new technologies, computer communication and simulation, increasing mobility and worldwide simultaneity. Some students simply took the educational curriculum as their point of departure for design, but were unable to transcend existing models.

Due to the extreme breadth of scope and complexity of task, students who had defined a limited yet clear focus succeeded in producing the most convincing projects. A metaphorical or poetic approach seemed more appropriate, than a technological or pragmatic one.

Project: 171717
Students: Jeremy Avellino, Amy Chorey, Cindy Cizmarik,
Christopher J. Golin, Richard Sanford
Teacher: Simon Koumijan
School: Philadelphia College of Textiles & Science, USA

The project uses the drafting table as the 'site' for a future architecture school, and
drafting artefacts - erasing shield, set-square, pencil sharpener et cetera - as the spaces
to discover the art and science of architecture. Resembling an archaeological
speculation on the use and function of 'archaic' implements, the project attempts an
imaginary reconstruction of the art and science of architecture using these implements
as inspiration. The traditional drafting table is dismantled and recomposed: the space
between the form and function of the implements is the space for imagination in which
the education of the architect occurs time and time again. Complementing modern
computer-oriented education, this 'school of architecture' introduces a physical and
personal component into the design process, and the act of drawing as the space to
discover the art and science of architecture.

The proposed metaphorical working table of the architect succeeds in evoking a rich and
meaningful imagery in its exploration of the central issues of architectural education:
the relation of thinking to making (creating a theoretical body of knowledge), methods
and tools of working and ideas, concept and execution, the mind and the hand, geometry
and composition, space and experience, making and material, 'Form' and 'Design'. By
presenting the 'future' working table as an alchemist's studio, the scheme also projects
images of future immaterial and simulation working methods. The project speaks about
the power of poetic images to condense a multitude of meanings and dimensions. The
power of the project lay in its ability to overcome and rise above the complexity of the
brief. Instead of providing an answer it offers an independent counter proposal, a tool, a
symbol with no policy. It is a metaphor, designed and elaborated with skill and
intelligence; evolving, suggesting and implying, but not prescribing.

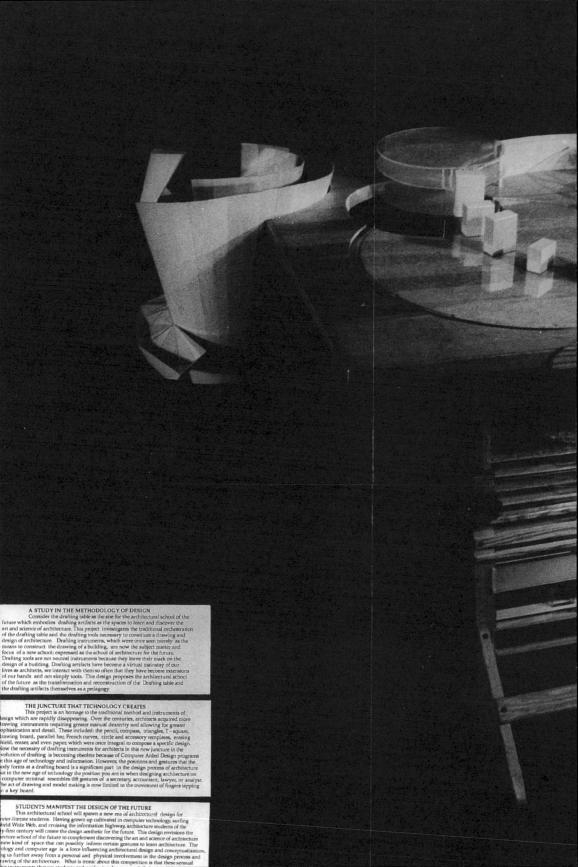

A STUDY IN THE METHODOLOGY OF DESIGN

Consider the drafting table as the site for the architectural school of the future which embodies drafting artifacts as the spaces to learn and discover the art and science of architecture. This project investigates the traditional orchestration of the drafting table and the drafting tools necessary to constitute a drawing and design of architecture. Drafting instruments, which were once seen merely as the means to construct the drawing of a building, are now the subject matter and focus of a new school; expressed as the school of architecture for the future. Drafting tools are not neutral instruments because they leave their mark on the design of a building. Drafting artifacts have become a virtual mainstay of our lives as architects, we interact with them so often that they have become extensions of our hands and not simply tools. This design proposes the architectural school of the future as the transformation and reconstruction of the Drafting table and the drafting artifacts themselves as a pedagogy.

THE JUNCTURE THAT TECHNOLOGY CREATES

This project is an homage to the traditional method and instruments of design which are rapidly disappearing. Over the centuries, architects acquired more drawing instruments requiring greater manual dexterity and allowing for greater sophistication and detail. These included: the pencil, compass, triangles, T - square, drawing board, parallel bar, French curves, circle and accessory templates, erasing shield, eraser, and even paper which were once integral to compose a specific design. Now the necessity of drafting instruments for architects in this new juncture in the evolution of drafting is becoming obsolete because of Computer Aided Design programs in this age of technology and information. However, the positions and gestures that the body forms at a drafting board is a significant part in the design process of architecture but in the new age of technology the position you are in when designing architecture on a computer terminal resembles the gestures of a secretary, accountant, lawyer, or analyst. The act of drawing and model making is now limited to the movement of fingers tapping on a key board.

STUDENTS MANIFEST THE DESIGN OF THE FUTURE

This architectural school will spawn a new era of architectural design for computer-literate students. Having grown up cultivated in computer technology, surfing the World Wide Web, and cruising the information highway, architecture students of the twenty-first century will create the design aesthetic for the future. This design envisions the architecture school of the future to complement discovering the art and science of architecture in a new kind of space that can possibly inform certain gestures to learn architecture. The technology and computer age is a force influencing architectural design and conceptualization, moving us further away from a personal and physical involvement in the design process and drawing of the architecture. What is ironic about this competition is that these sensual

A Study in the Methodology of Design

Consider the drafting table as the site for the architectural school of the future which embodies drafting artefacts as the spaces to learn and discover the art and science of architecture. This project investigates the traditional orchestration of the drafting table and the drafting tools necessary to constitute a drawing and design of architecture. Drafting instruments, which were once seen merely as the means to construct the drawing of a building, are now the subject matter and focus of a new school; expressed as the school of architecture for the future. Drafting tools are not neutral elements because they leave their mark on the design of a building. Drafting artefacts have become a virtual mainstay of our lives as architects, we interact with them so often that they have become extensions of our hands and not simple tools. This design proposes the architectural school of the future as the transformation and reconstruction of the drafting table and the drafting artefacts themselves as a pedagogy.

The Juncture that Technology Creates

This project is a homage to the traditional method and instruments of design which are rapidly disappearing. Over the centuries, architects acquired more drawing instruments requiring greater manual dexterity and allowing for greater sophistication and detail. These included: the pencil, compass, triangles, T-square, drawing board, parallel bar, French curves, circle and accessory templates, erasing shield, eraser, and even paper, which were once integral to compose a specific design. Now the necessity of drawing instruments for architects in this new juncture in the evolution of drafting is becoming obsolete because of Computer Aided Design programs in this age of technology and information. However, while the positions and gestures that the body forms at a drafting board play a significant part in the design process of architecture, in the computer age the position you are in when designing architecture on a computer terminal resembles that of a secretary, accountant, lawyer, or analyst. The act of drawing and model making is now limited to the movement of fingers tapping on a key board.

Students Manifest the Design of the Future

This architectural school will spawn a new era of architectural design for computer-literate students. Having grown up cultivated in computer technology, surfing on the World Wide Web, and cruising the information highway, architecture students of the twenty-first century will create the design aesthetic for the future. This design envisions an architectural school of the future to complement discovering the science and art of architecture through a new kind of space that may generate certain gestures for learning architecture. The technology of the computer age is a force influencing architectural design and conceptualisation, leading us further away from a personal and physical involvement in the design process and the drawing of architecture. What is ironic about this competition is that these sensual drafting instruments, that we students and professionals use on a daily basis, will be ousted before the architectural school of the future is theoretically realised.

50

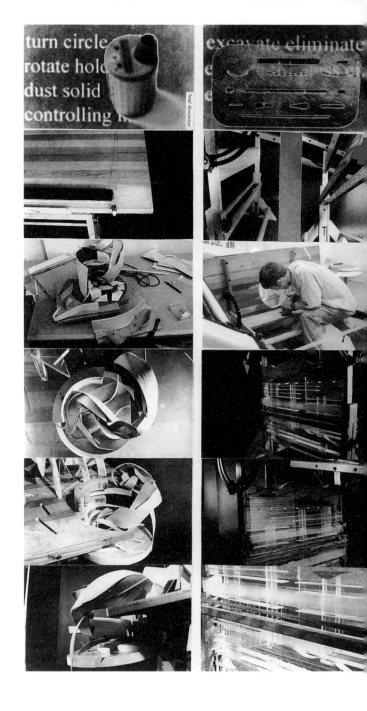

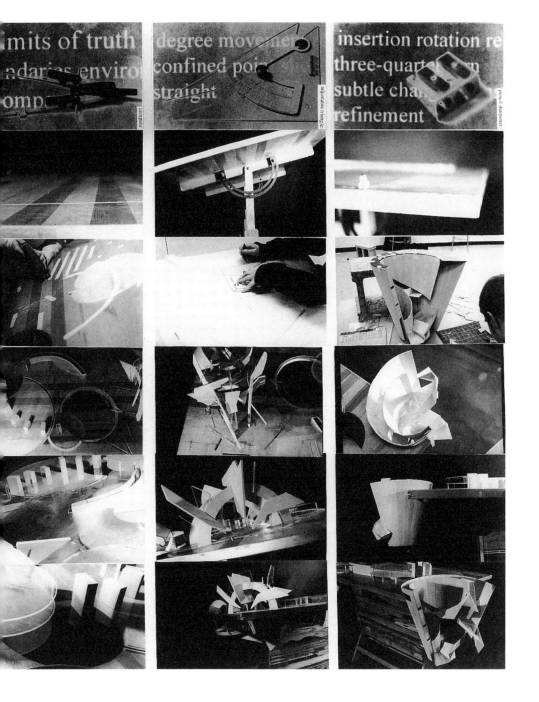

mits of truth
ndaries enviro
omp

compass

degree moveme
confined po
straight

adjustable triangle

insertion rotation re
three-quarter
subtle cha
refinement

pencil sharpener

Honourable Mention

Project: 9nueve
Student: Cristina Diaz-Moreno
School: Universidad Politecnica de Madrid, Spain (exchange student at the Bartlett School of Architecture and Planning, London, United Kingdom)

The Future

This design proposes a large, open landscape-like space to house the future school of architecture. The curriculum is outlined in a five-point statement on architectural training. The project is a metaphorical evocation rather than a realistic architectural proposal. The text expresses a valid concern for the future of the profession of architecture.

Although the project fails somewhat to walk the thin line between the schematic, the programmatic, the concrete and the idea, the jury found the design of sufficient quality to join the group of noteworthy entries.

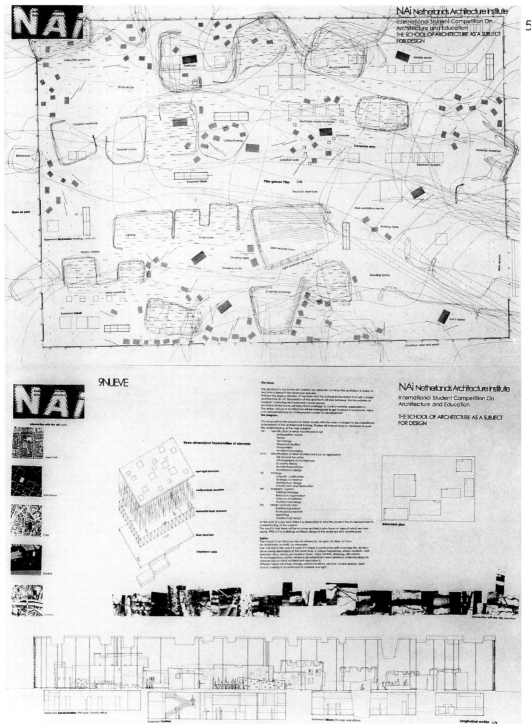

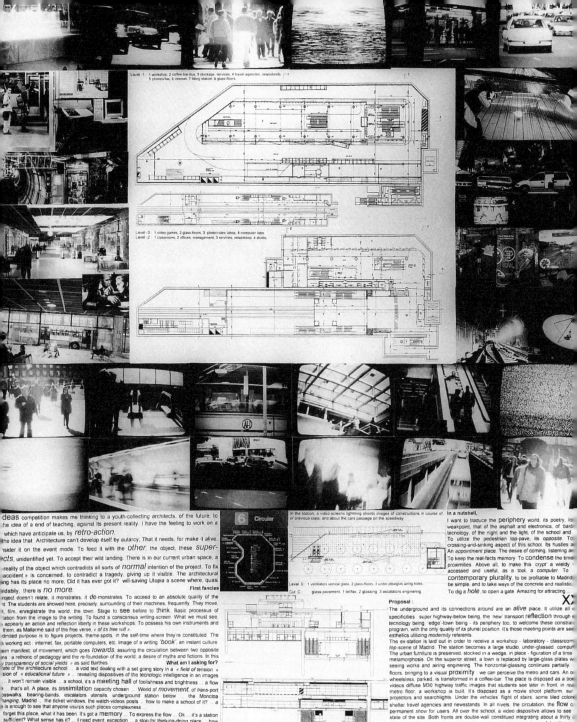

Level -1 : 1 workshop, 2 coffee-bar-bus, 3 stockage, services, 4 travel agencies, newsstands. c
5 phones/fax, 6 internet, 7 filling station, 8 glass-floors.

Level -3 : 1 video games, 2 glass-floors, 3 photo/video labos, 4 computer labo.
Level -2 : 1 classrooms, 2 offices, management, 3 services, newsstand, 4 studio.

...deas competition makes me thinking to a youth-collecting architects, of the future, to
...he idea of a end of teaching, against its present reality, I have the feeling to work on a
... which have anticipate us, by *retro-action*.
...the idea that Architecture can't develop itself by autarcy, That it needs, for make it alive,
...sider it on the event mode. To feed it with the *other*, the object, these *super-*
...cts, unidentified yet. To accept their wild landing. There is in our current urban space, a
...reality of the object which contradicts all sorts of *normal* intention of the project. To fix
...accident » is concerned, to contradict a tragedy, giving up it visible. The architectural
...ing has its place no more, Did it has ever got it? will-saving Utopia a scene where, quasi
...eidably, there is *no more*.

First fancies

...roject doesn't relate, it monstrates, it *de*-monstrates. To acceed to an absolute quality of the
...nt. The students are showed here, precisely, surrounding of their machines, frequently. They move,
...lation from the image to the writing. To found a conscensus writing-screen. What we must see,
... appearly an action and reflection liberty in these workshops. To possess his own instruments and
...them, as Mallarmé said of the free verse, « of its free will »
...dmited purpose is to figure projects, theme-spots, in the self-time where they're constituted.
...s working act : internet, fax, portable computers, etc. Image of a writing '*book*', an instant culture.
...ern manifest, of movement, which goes *towards*, assuring the circulation between two opposite
...s a rhetoric of pedagogy and the re-foundation of the world, a desire of myths and fictions. In this
... transparency of social yields » as said Barthes.

What am I asking for?

...ate of the architecture school ... a void text dealing with a set going story in a « *field of tension* »
...sion of « *educational future* » ... revealing dispositives of the tecnologic intelligence in an images
...it won't remain visible ... a school, it's a **meeting hall** of foolishness and brightness ... a flow
...that's all. A place, its **assimilation** capacity chosen ... World of **movement**, of trans-port
...osswalks, bearing-bands, escalators utensils, underground station below ... the Moncloa
...hanging, Madrid ... the ticket windows, the watch-videos posts ... how to make a school of it? ... a
...s enough to see that anyone usurps such places complexness ...
...forget this place, what it has been. It's got a **memory** ... To express the flow ... Ok ... it's a station
...sufficient? What sense has it? ... I need **event**, exception ... a stop-for-thinking-doing place ... how
...sing that?
...chool is situated at the periphery of Madrid, in jonction of the M30 highway, the middle town and the
...sity ... road world, of transport, of daily ... universe of signs so banalized, of an so ambiant
...nity, they became invisible. In an amnesia of glance. What pedestrians see on top? from the
... The escalators slice ... bus headlights ... people are walking, running, late ... A bolh-urban
...nds **interface**: between a big town, its twinkling trades, its maintained streets and periphery, its
...fallows, its waste ground, highway bands To live in this interface, in a unsettled situation,
...ays.
...pot, asphalted desert, trans-signed, trans-coded, its tramed lightning, its mathematic technics. I
...now from where emerge this unvolontary esthetic. It means at the firsts Scorcese's movies, the
...tcher's, s... All is on its own place ... security, airing, lights ... it stays [1. *Mean streets*, M.Scorcese, 1974.
...breath it the void, the spirit ... a school, what ! [2. *Seven*, D. Fintcher, 1996.
...w to live a station? a halt? with the underground below? ... a « field of tension » ... yes, of course!
...s sense ... but, how to live a sense?

6 Circular

In the station, a video-screens lightning shoots images of constructions in course of, of previous state, and about the cars passage on the speedway

Level 0 : 1 ventilators vertical glass, 2 glass-floors, 3 under-glasglins airing holes.
Cut C : glass-pavement, 1 teil/fax, 2 glassing, 3 escalators enginering

Cut E : 1 airing, 2 filling station, 3 ventilators, 4 studio.

Cut A : 1 glassing lawn, 2 ventilators.

In a nutshell,

The underground and its connections around are an *alive* place. It utilize all
weakpoint, that of the asphalt and electronics, of barb
tecnology, of the right and the light, of the school and
To utilize the pedestrian top-over, its opposite. To
crossing-and-sinking aspect of this school, its hustles an
An *appointment* place. The desire of coming, listening an
To keep the real-facts memory To **condense the time**
proximities. Above all, to make this *crypt* a wieldy
accessed and useful, as a tool, a *computer*. To
contemporary plurality, to be profitable to Madrid
be simple, and to take ways of the concrete and realistic
To dig a *hole*, to open a gate. Amazing for attracting ...

X.

Proposal :

The underground and its connections around are an *alive* place. It utilize all
specificities super highway-below being, the new transport *reflection* through
tecnology being, edge -town being - its periphery too, to welcome these constrain
program, with the only quality of its plural position. It's those meeting points are see
esthetics utilizing *modernity* referents.
The ex-station is laid out in order to receive a workshop - laboratory - classroom
top-scene of Madrid. The station becomes a large studio, under-glassed, compu
The urban furniture is preserved, stocked in a wedge, in place - figuration of a time
metamorphosis. On the superior street, a lown is replaced by large-glass plates w
seeing works and airing enginering. The horizontal-glassing continues partially
floors, bringing to a visual *proximity* we can perceive the metro and cars. An o
wheeless, parked, is transformed in a coffee-bar. The place is disposed as a bo
videos diffuse M30 highway traffic images that students see later in front, in rea
metro floor, a workshop is built. It's disposed as a movie shoot platform, sur
projectors and searchlights. Under the vehicles flight of stairs, some tiled colore
shelter travel agencies and newsstands. In all nivels, the circulation, the *flow* c
permanent *show* for users. All over the school, a video dispositive allows to see
state of the site. Both fronts are double-wall constituted integrating about a thirty
fax posts receving signs of the world (and others schools) Work of *ubiquity*, co
time

Project: xxxll
Student: Guillaume de Malet Roquefort
School: Université de Bordeaux, France (exchange student at
the Universidad Complutense de Madrid, Spain)

An existing metro station in Madrid is the site for this school
design. The intention is to place architectural education in the midst of
urban life and activity, thus negating its usual academic isolation. The
student utilises an extremely modern condition, the non-spaces of the
contemporary urban periphery and their 'asphalt and electronics', as the
context for academic pursuit.

The fact that the original function of the station appears to be eliminated
diminishes the strength of the concept. Nevertheless the fascination with
urban processes and academic life is noteworthy, if still greatly
undeveloped.

Honourable Mention

Project: 160196
Student: Svetlana Nekrasova
School: Ural Academy of Architecture & Art, Russia

Architectural Metamorphosis

The project uses the metamorphosis of the caterpillar into the butterfly as an analogy of the education of an architect: the stages are larva (prospective student); young caterpillar (beginning); developing caterpillar (learning - as larva differ in quality, so too do students; three types are distinguished - talent and strong background skill, talented but lazy and average with good background skills); the cocoon phase (experience in the design studio); and the final stage as a fully-fledged butterfly (graduation and practice).

The proposal is a childlike metaphor of the method and purpose of architectural education. The innocence of the metaphor depicts the timeless essence of education rather than presenting a futuristic vision. The care and devotion with which this metaphor is depicted, and the insight it reveals into the personal act of learning, something that should be present in every student devoted to the discipline, made this a memorable scheme.

~daidu jilbad

edifice grunge:

anamorphosis

iso

ijakifers iso dynamic

post woto node

neoelectronic

isomorphic architect

educom server

cleave subgeo

ilacature

anti isoclinal

extrinsic (domain)

sub_otu kutan

ijakifers iso dynamic

extrinsic (domain)

edifice grunge:

sub_otu kutan

~ daidu jilbad

isomorphic architect

Project: 954184
Student: Christine Beveridge
School: Curtin University of Technology, Western Australia,
Australia

This apocalyptic, anti-Utopian future scenario envisages
life and education in the wake of an environmental catastrophe. The
earth's surface having been rendered uninhabitable, education goes
underground, contained in 'subgeo enviroarchitecture'. Each
'enviroversity' is set in a location regenerated from the wastelands of the
late 20th century. The realm of architecture, and thus architectural
education, is adapted to the new circumstances - a concern with the impact
on the earth's resources, reclamation, sustainable lifestyles, efficient
transport and the 'design of spaces of immense beauty underground'. The
studios focus on sensory perception, spatial awareness, colour, tactility,
and olfactory and audio enhancement.

The vision could have been developed in further literary detail, but the
project is noteworthy as a reminder of possible disasters and manner in
which architecture responds to and overcomes such crises.

Honourable Mention

Project: torens
Students: Evelyn van der Ploeg, Henri van Bennekom
School: University of Technology Delft, Netherlands

Towers

The project proposes that the school be housed in a network of identical towers placed in various locations; city centre, urban periphery, residential areas, et cetera. The school can occupy the towers in various ways: each tower for a study year, a discipline, or a mixture of creative subjects. The act of travelling from tower to tower allows students an opportunity for 'reflection', and a chance to engage with the built environment and fellow citizens. The combination of a strong primal form, 'a form which was always there and will always be there', with different interior designs and placed in different contexts enables students to study the interaction of building and surroundings, interior and exterior.

The network of towers appears arbitrary and could have been developed into a conceptually motivated structure juxtaposed on the urban structure. Although still naive and underdeveloped in its architectural translation and expression, it was considered the most striking project of it kind.

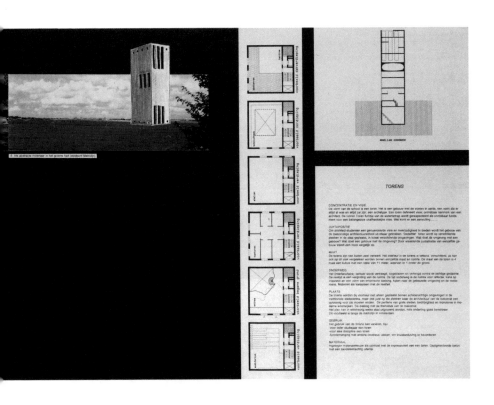

http://www.bitzfill.uk

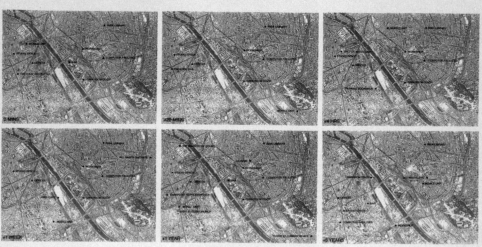

g24k3

g24k31

Project: g24k31
Students: Kate Darby, Geoff Brocklehurst
School: Architectural Association, London, United Kingdom

A School of Architecture for the Future

Current aspects of urban planning, economics and the electronic highway are exploited to define the 'ephemeral' architectural school of the future. This school is a decentralised organisation utilising underused or vacant spaces in the city as temporary sites. The school's formal organisation is adapted accordingly to the flexible, invisible system. It is a framework in which both students and staff operate with no defined hierarchy. The Internet becomes the spine and public profile of the school, where curricula and activities are communicated.

The idea of utilising existing unused urban sites is valid, but should have been developed in more detail. The proposal remains vague and has a haphazard character. The idea could have been more realistically and seductively presented, but has nonetheless a strong underlying concept.

'25% of London's buildings are empty at any one time. They are unused buildings such as offices awaiting occupancy, shops to let, empty sites, derelict industrial buildings. They are also underused buildings such as cinemas, night clubs and parking lots. ... A team of administrators would scout for temporary sites in which to house the activities of the organisation and co-ordinate its activities by updating and maintaining the events list on the Internet and balancing the numbers of tutors and students. Building maintenance and audio visual resources would be combined in mobile units which would prepare temporary sites for use. All tutors would be part time and employed on annual contracts.... Public libraries and specialist architectural libraries , book shops, graphic suppliers and reprographic facilities are permanently available in cities independent of schools of architecture, as are bars and restaurants...'

Honourable Mention

Project: kaukei
Students: Oleum Chan Yung, Kelvin Kan Yu Sing
School: University of Hong Kong, Hong Kong

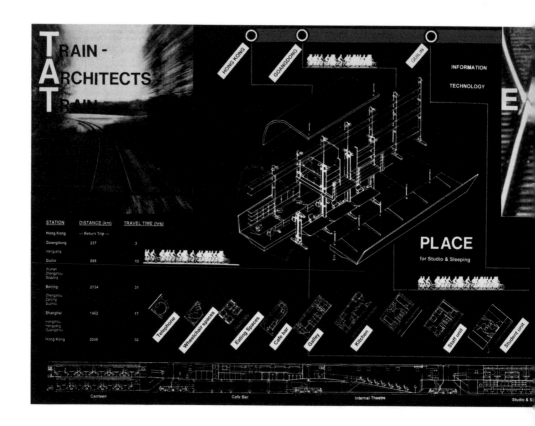

A double-deck train travelling from Hong Kong to the main provinces of China is the setting for this school of architecture. All necessities for study are contained in the adjustable train, such as its transformation into a lecture theatre when standing still. By journeying from place to place the school serves as a source of information for the inhabitants encountered along the way, a vehicle for cultural exchange and an environment for study.

'Experience, exposure and exchange' is the valid aim of bringing education into contact with the realities of rural life and to stimulate a broader view of the profession's role. The technical solutions to the various facilities within the confines of a standard train carriage have been designed with considerable skill.

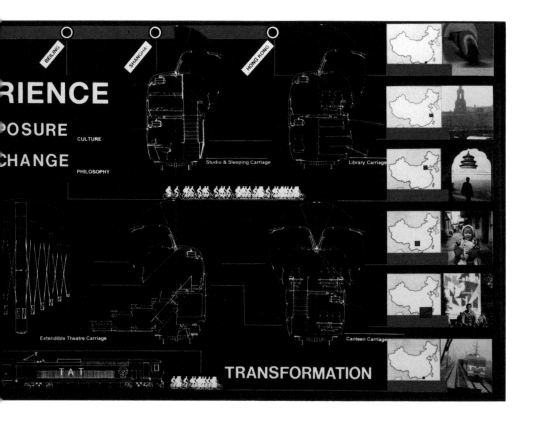

Honourable Mention

Project: mus965
Students: Yahya Al Tahan Aliraqi, Mustafa Salman Alomran
School: University of East London, United Kingdom

Living Workshop

A ship arrives in Japan with a cargo of fruit from Brazil and is converted
for the return journey into a ship carrying Japanese cars. This project sets
out to explore the benefits of stronger links between architecture and other
technological fields and sciences. The school is a 'Link Base' with
industries such as the space, military and shipping industries. The global
network of 'building stations' are workshop locations where students can
'participate, observe, learn, test and study real problems'. Each station
consists of a testing programme lab, product information bank, digital 3-D
workshop, media station and 'stress purification cell for young stressed
students who need a haven from daily stress'.

The proposal is a technological Utopia related to the futuristic visions of
the late 1960s. The proposed 'Mecca School of Architecture' emphasises
workshop activities, experimentation, flexibility and virtual mobility.
However seductive the inspiration for this design, the project remains
vague about how the link is established with other technological fields and
sciences.

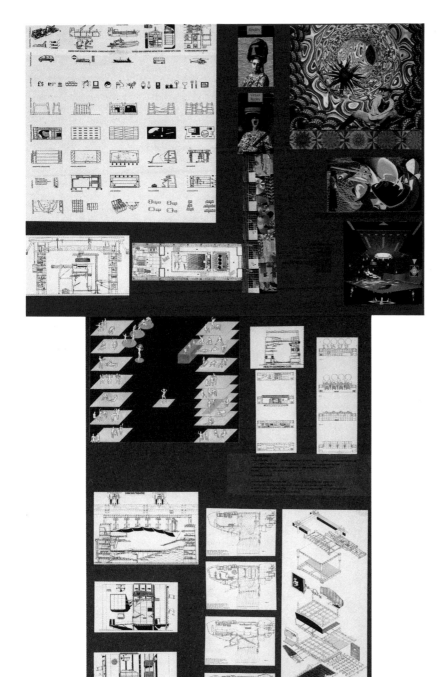

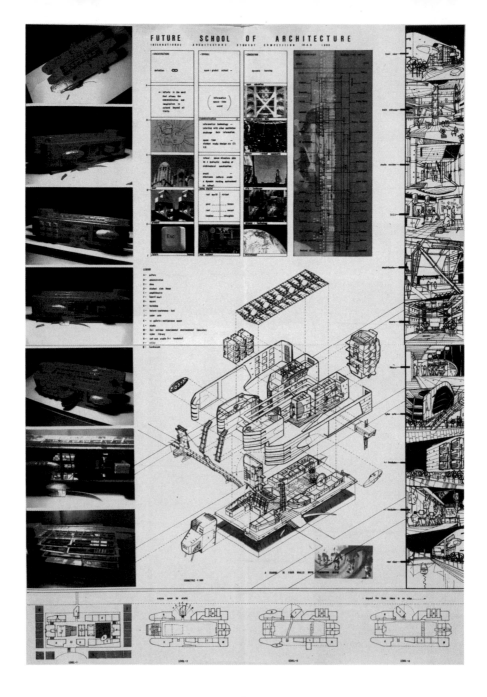

FUTURE SCHOOL OF ARCHITECTURE

Instruction and Distraction

Arthur Wortmann

It is scarcely possible to imagine a more didactically justified competition then this one for the architecture school of the future. Students were obliged to reflect on their own situation, to evaluate the education being offered them and to ask themselves questions about their role in society. What could be more appropriate to an educational programme than a task that stimulates such a raising of consciousness? The link between the design to be submitted and the vision, moreover, underlined the importance of a conceptual approach to design. Further, the competition can be looked upon as a survey of current educational models and a search for alternatives. So not only the students, but also the schools and the very discipline of architecture had something to gain from this competition.

There is no doubt that viewed as an international event the competition was a success, considering the large number of competitors from many countries. The question is of course whether the quantitative and geographic success of the design competition guaranteed high-quality entries and valid ideas with which schools of architecture can face the future. The following classification of entries gives some idea of the directions in which the participants sought solutions to the task at hand.

Fun and games

As in every (student) competition, the first of our categories comprises the frivolous entries. For the most part, these are proposals by students who, having failed to make any headway with the task, have sought a contrived way out of their impasse. For example, one entrant felt compelled to submit a bar code (Andrea Petrecca, Pescara, Italy); another, with the watchword 'we shall not accommodate ourselves before others', refused to produce a design at all (Roderico Ibanez, Los Angeles, US), and a third student presented a few vague pencil lines, because 'the future is still vague' (Pedro Marta, Delft, Netherlands). The many collages of visual material, relevant or otherwise, also fall within this category. Here, the design process failed to progress beyond illustrating a brainstorming session. Only a very few of the flippant entries were accompanied by a well-groomed presentation or a meaningful design account, with the aim of

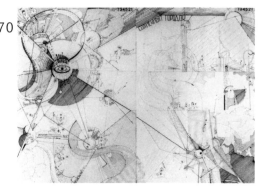

briefly capturing the attention after all. One example is the entry submitted by Irina Konoshencko (Yekaterinburg, Russia), which is populated by spectres and features an architecture school on Pluto, with departments on the other planets in our solar system.

Alternatives, metaphors, neutral structures

A second category comprises entrants who designed an alternative to their own school of architecture. For the most part, these are realistic plans, responding to a specific setting and accommodating a traditional programme. And although this approach has here and there resulted in some superb buildings, most lack the universal nature one might expect from the results of an ideas competition. At certain architecture schools, it appears that the teachers themselves have added a new site to the brief (for didactic reasons?). A notable example is the series of designs for a school in Venice, submitted by, would you believe, the University of Kentucky.

The third category contains the metaphorical plans. The school is depicted as an (ivory) tower or a bridge (literally and figuratively); the architectural training is represented as a quest or as an emergence from a pupal stage (a caterpillar becomes a butterfly in the extraordinary drawing submitted by Svetlana Nekrasova of Yekaterinburg, Russia); architecture is reduced to a musical note (one of the four entries by the team from Pescara, Italy - Simone Barlafante, Monica Maggi, Francesco Polcini, Barbara Serrani and Tesco Staffilani - follows Schopenhauer's thesis that architecture is frozen music) or to a geometric pattern with a supposed divine significance.

The schemes containing neutral buildings or structures can be regarded as a fourth category. If the buildings in the previous two categories are too specific, either because of the setting or the brief, or because of the meaning of the formal idiom, these designs are too

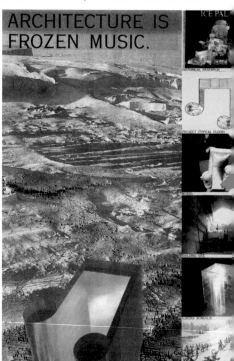

general to be able to fulfil an inspiring or exemplary function. This category also includes the entrants who believe that a school of architecture (like any other function) can be housed in the nearest vacant building, making it quite unnecessary to design new structures. Be that as it may, one wonders why they bothered submitting an entry at all.

Prototypes

One of the most interesting categories comprises what we could call prototypical plans. These seek an equilibrium between the general and the specific. The architecture school is divided into distinct elements or activities, with suitable accommodation then being designed for each. Rolf Bekker (Amsterdam, Netherlands) devised constructional schemes derived from the way in which an auditorium, library or studio functions. These schemes could serve as a guiding principle for the design in each new building task. Unfortunately, Bekker's own solution was disappointing. The entry submitted by Tatiana Boudantseva (Yekaterinburg, Russia) contains a more spiritual division: concentrated thought, personal development, original idea and historical consciousness are given shape in an upside-down pyramid, a cylinder, an egg and a mansion respectively - four volumes which together constitute the new school. Rob Hendriks (Amsterdam, Netherlands) presented a tripartite division: an underground data level and a raised 'laboratory' (with shed roof), separated from each other by an exterior space which represents 'the world'. The design is facetiously described as 'the first open-air school for the healthy architecture student'. Siiri Vallner and Hanno Grossschmidt (Tallinn, Estonia) designed a building whose four storeys distinguish between a social level, a group level, an individual level and a mental level. Yet using the placement of the furniture to flesh out this idea is a fairly prosaic solution. Maxim Vitalievich Lukyanov (Dnepropetrovsk, Ukraine) offered a more poetic alternative. In a school with a four-layered organization basic knowledge is provided on a staircase, professional skills are taught in the labyrinth, philosophical reflection takes place in the 'space of sensibility', and in the 'space of dialogue' students have to work out their own philosophy. The

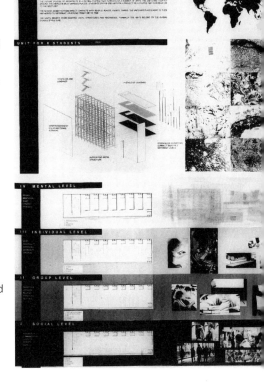

presentation of this plan was a cross between a collage of motifs from the art of painting and a somewhat disappointing architectural model.

Experience

A sixth category of entrants sought the solution to the design task in experience. They design for their fellow man, whom they regard as a collection of senses. For them designing is giving form to a spatial experience, and a school of architecture just has to be the grooviest spatial experience of all. So the design task was taken by these students as a pretext for interpreting the question as to what constitutes an inspiring spatial experience along highly personal lines. An entrant from Mexico, for example, submitted a building which sets out to recreate the experience of a bungee jump (Diana Ramirez Jasso of Guadelajara), and one from Russia presented a design for a school as a labyrinth (Matvey Malakhov of Novo-Sadovaya). There were innumerable more or less 'deconstructivist' entries which dynamically distorted designs by Libeskind, Morphosis, Tschumi, Eisenman and Koolhaas. The entrants obviously had a great time making them, but their designs are far too obtrusive to be able to function as models for an architecture school of the future.

The mobile school

The big hit of the competition is the seventh category. Here too, the preoccupation is with spatial experience, only this time this is not sought in the school itself, but in the world around us. If one lesson can be drawn from this competition it is that students would like nothing better than a mobile school of architecture. Every possibility is investigated: there are entries for schools in nomad camps of containers, in demountable study cells, in cars, in buses, in lorries, in metros, in trains, in boats, in submarines... And in addition to the students who designed these mobile schools, there are those who sought their solution to the design task in a curriculum to be taught at various locations around the world. Scott McCarthy (Houston, US), for example, envisages a six-year programme in which students attend successive one-year courses in Washington, Sydney, Porto Alegre, Johannesburg, Calcutta and Paris. He himself designed a standard tower block providing accommodation for students and educational facilities in each of these cities.

Notably, in many of these entries displacement is an end in itself, with no effort at all being made to weigh up the advantages and disadvantages of a mobile school or a travelling student curriculum. No one seems to doubt the edifying qualities of travelling. In only a few cases are programme components deliberately linked to specific locations.

A number of entries with a strong social dimension present a special type of mobile architecture school. In one of the entries from Lebanon, for example, the school is a social condenser travelling through impoverished regions and combining the learning process with practical experience and a very direct form of social contribution (Nathalie Mahfoud, Beirut).

Public domain and seclusion

Another group, the eighth category, also seeks contact with the outside world, but its members limit themselves to their familiar environment. They are not concerned with the travelling student, but rather with intensifying interaction with the 'real' world. The barriers between school and city, between institute and society, need to be broken down. Students don't need to be improved, much has already been achieved if they can be prevented from becoming blunted - this seems to be the modest underlying idea. This gives rise to an assortment of 'open-door schools'; for example, schools whose buildings are arranged around a forum, a public square where students and the public can learn to understand each other (Shawn Corbin, Gatesville, US).

Yet according to another category of entrants, seclusion is essential. The college is a fortress or a sequestered boarding school. Some even seek isolation in outer space; in a rocket (Elena Smirnova, Dnepropetrovsk, Ukraine), a

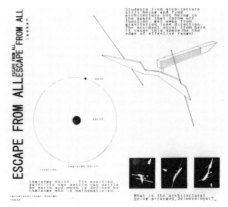

satellite (Hiroshi Iseya, Chiba, Japan) or a space station (Michael Nolen, Houston, US). A large group, however, seeks seclusion in virtual space. Remarkably, very few entrants give their reasons for this. Is it for practical purposes (making it easy on yourself)? For ecological reasons (fewer environmentally-unfriendly journeys)? It seems that many students used the science-fiction content of the design task - a vision of the school of the future - as a pretext to give free rein to their fantasy. Oiva Vesa and Jussi Kallioxpuska (Oulu, Finland) designed something that looks like a fabulous home screen of a virtual architecture school with a spatial structure (although the design report gives the impression that the building does indeed have a material presence). Other devotees of the electronic revolution (Keith Brown and Eric Mayne, Milwaukee, US) already imagine the architectural history program being downloaded, and envisage themselves getting cut off from the rest of their class on a virtual excursion to Chicago.

Of a very different order are the schemes by entrants who seek seclusion in nature. For them, it is our pernicious culture we need to escape from. These entrants believe that the world is going in the wrong direction and that students of architecture must take the lead in seeking a solution. Whether they will succeed by, say, building a school in the trees to study ecology (James Mol, Houston, US) is doubtful. The designers of one Chinese entry were pessimistic enough to depict a school looking like a giant mushroom in a lunar landscape, for use after the Third World War (Keyan Li and Rui Du, Changchun-Jilin, China).

Hors catégorie

The tenth and last category is, indeed, the hors catégorie: the entries which, because of their vision and originality, cannot be categorized. One is the comic strip by Olivier Troost (Antwerp, Belgium) which admittedly tells us

very little about his views on architectural education in the future, but does have a marvellous expressive power. Equally fascinating are the entries submitted by a team from Philadelphia (Jeremy Avellino, Amy Chorey, Cindy Cizmarik, Christopher

Golin and Richard Sanford, US), who didn't design a school, but an unusual drawing table in homage to traditional design methods and tools, and the wonderful suitcase by Olivier Ottevaere and Serge Gascon (Montreal, Canada), containing an assortment of incomprehensible instruments. As superb as it is inimitable is the idea and presentation submitted by Anna Ansimovo (Yekaterinburg, Russia). She sees the student as the button which, by means of the needle (the subject matter taught) and the thread (education), becomes operational and is then able to establish temporary connections. Another original idea was that submitted by Saskia Kloosterboer (Paris, France). She pictures the school as a spatial object with three ribs which, seen from a certain position, produces the paradoxical image of a physically impossible triangle, familiar to us from the drawings of M.C. Escher. Her

accompanying statement betrays a certain aversion to the brief: 'The production of an ideal ... cannot be but an optical ideal and a visual realization of a banalized utopia ...'. Unfortunately, the crucial, 'optically ideal' viewpoint plays no role in the design variants she produced, so that the theoretical content would fail to show through in practice.

What is so reassuring about the competition is the ease with which entrants succeeded in interpreting the brief to suit their own purposes. Of course the competition failed to yield the well-thought-out alternative educational models the organizers, the jury and the participating educational establishments had perhaps hoped for. You couldn't expect the entrants to be interested in that. Most are still in the early stages of their training and it is essential that they are given the opportunity to experiment and pursue their own pet projects. A competition provides students with the chance to do just this, to escape from the demands and conventions of their training and do their own thing. A competition such as this provides an element of distraction, that essential dose of freedom. The 424 entries should be seen primarily in this light: 424 attempts to find a personal direction in the quest called architectural education.

This text is an abridged version of an article published in **Archis** no. 9, 1996.

A worldwide panorama of architectural education

Fred Feddes

In setting this international student competition the expectations were modest. The poster with the announcement and the regulations was indeed sent to 856 educational institutions, while the announcement also appeared in Archis, Domus and other journals, but it could not be estimated to what extent the task would appeal to students and teachers. The organizers claimed they would be content with sixty to a hundred entries.

In the succeeding months it became clear that the interest was much greater. About a thousand requests for information and registration came in, from such diverse countries as Algeria, Chile and Pakistan. The stopwatch finally clicked at 424 entries. Almost two thirds gave a single designer's name, the rest were submitted by teams of two to twenty people. A total of 661 students worked on the designs.

There were some shifts between registration and entry. In the beginning dozens of request for information and registration came form Brazil, and ultimately only eight entries. The entries announced from Argentina and Chile also failed to materialize.

It is not only the entries which show great diversity, but also the administration. Therefore some preliminary remarks on the data given in this article:
- Not all entries contained sufficient information about the sender; it is possible that some commentaries were lost in the post. It was often possible to track down this information. But two entries were known only by their codes: '314R50' and 'Fossilis'. The data therefore are based on 422 traceable entries and 160 institutions.
- The name of the institution was sometimes given in the native language, sometimes in English; occasionally different English translations of the same name cropped up. Sometimes the name of the overall educational organization was given, for example the university, sometimes that of a faculty or department, sometimes both. The survey attempts to offer a simple and if possible, accurate picture.
- Unfortunately the participants were not asked for their sex. Nevertheless there is an impression that a considerable proportion of the entrants are women. For example, about half the Lebanese entries are by women.
- Nor were entrants required to state their nationality. This means it is not

possible to make generalizations about the extent of educational migration. The inventory of countries is therefore based as much as possible on the country where the education is based. A classification in terms of nationality would probably have led to a greater number of countries. For example, there are two entries by Irish students studying in Germany, while another entrant gives a home address in the United Arab Emirates and a school address in the USA. Furthermore, exchange programmes leave their traces, for example where Spanish students spend a year in British or German institutions. A Finnish entrant studies in Budapest, lives in Barcelona and for her design chose a Swedish location. The four participating students from the Danish International Study Program all live in the USA or Canada. However, these cases, striking though they are, seem to be the exception rather than the rule.

- Entries which came in after the closing date have also been incorporated into the survey tables. The provisional last entry reached the NAi on 6 June. It cannot be ruled out that somewhere in the world future schools of architecture are still waiting in post offices or airport depots for their long journey to Rotterdam.

Countries

The entries come from 42 countries, throughout the world. Naturally, almost all Western European countries and the USA are represented. The USA provided the largest number: 66. The number of Dutch entries -55- is somewhat misleading, as more than a quarter come from the Faculty of Art and Cultural Sciences of the Erasmus University, which does not offer a design course but a general introduction to architectural history. Countries renowned for participating in competitions, such as Italy and Great Britain are well represented, as is Belgium, while the number of entries from Germany and France is rather low.

What is striking is the interest from Russia (27), Australia (25), Lebanon (21) and China (16), as well as entries from, among others, Guatemala, Hong Kong, the Ukraine, Kazakhstan and Iran. The geographic distribution conjures up the image of almost a thousand posters whirling around the world from Rotterdam to end up in places which the organizers could never have suspected beforehand.

A distribution in terms of continents shows that Europe provided the largest number of entries (194), even though this is less than might be expected from a European initiative like this competition. Africa is under-represented, even when the number of entries is compared to the numbers of schools of architecture per continent, and Australia is over-represented. It is also noticeable that the majority of the Russian entries (23) come from the Asiatic part of that country.

Educational institutions

The entrants are registered in 160 different courses. The early course years in particular are heavily represented. Ninety percent of the participants are undergraduate students, the rest are graduate or post-graduate students. A number of colleges treated the competition task as part of the training. That was the case for example in the Ural Academy of Architecture and Arts in Jekaterinaburg, from whence came 17 entries, and courses in Houston, Perth and Beirut; in this last city two courses made the task part of the curriculum. All nine entries from Hong Kong come from a single institution.

Some sent photos of models with their entries, an indication that a lot of time was spent on them. A group of American students combined the task with their impressions of a study trip to Venice. Tackling the task in a college did not necessarily lead to a large number of entries. For example, Wang Judong of the Shandong Institute of Architecture and Engineering in Jinan (China) wrote about the working method used there: 'The president of our college and dean of architecture department paid much attention to it. We think it is very important to us to improve the ability of architect design and to have good academic chance to communicate with the institute of architecture in other countries. In order to take part in the competition, we've selected two top students and arranged three excellent tutors to guide them.'

From other countries, such as Great Britain, Italy, Germany and Brazil, there were almost exclusively individual entries. The makers of the 16 German entries, for example, are studying at eleven different courses. In the Netherlands too it would appear that hardly any attention was paid to the competition in the educational context, except at the Erasmus University. From the United States, 21 courses nation-wide are represented; three of those, in Houston, Raleigh and Lexington, produced about half the American entries.

Comparison with jury assessment

One of the 21 plans on which the jury's deliberations concentrated, was the proposal by Marco Chan Pan Hang and Eddie Nip Kan Chong from Hong Kong for a travelling school of architecture, 'Anywhere can be School of

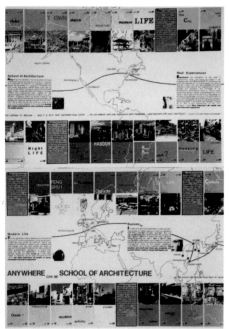

Architecture'. The Hong Kong students of the imagined school spend a year in China, then Europe, USA and Japan, and in the fifth year return to Hong Kong.

'This is characteristic of how a twenty-year-old thinks about "where it's at in the work of architecture"', remarked one of the jury members about this plan: where it's at is Western Europe, the USA, and Southeast Asia.

Ironically enough, that image is confirmed by the judgment of the same jury. The winner comes from the United states. Of the eight plans with an honourable mention five come from Western Europe, one from Australia and one from Hong Kong, with just one entry from Russia somewhat upsetting the image. Of the twelve other projects which were discussed at length, one came from Russia, and the rest came once again from Western Europe (6), the USA (2) and Hong Kong (3). Thus, fewer than 10 percent of the plans discussed in detail by the jury came from outside the three regions mentioned (plus Australia), as against 30 percent of all entries. The Hong Kong architectural courses were remarkably successful: four of the nine entries made it to the final round.

Education and architecture

After its tour of the plans the jury claimed to be 'shocked' by the low standard of the entries. They had encountered hardly any 'mature' plans; plenty of 'empty imagery', easy utopias, manifestos and cliches. Many entrants 'are trying to be clever without being intelligent'. 'None of them', sighed a jury member, 'is a new Rem.'

The question is whether this shock - apparently the jury had other expectations - is justified. The competition was very accessible: every student of architecture could participate and the formulation of the task left a lot of freedom. This meant that one could expect a cross section of education in which brilliant and rambling, first year and postgraduate, mature and tyro appear in ratios which perhaps chime with the reality of architectural education as provided worldwide by almost 900 institutions to tens of thousands of students.

Education is a dipping rhyme of (auto)selection after the gate. Every year, many thousands of young people begin training as architects. Some drop out along the way, some do other work after training, a considerable number will spend their working lives in anonymity, a small proportion will pursue postgraduate training. Only a handful are recognised as 'important' architects, according to whatever criterion. The pattern is that of the Olympic Games, where only a few hundred of the ten thousand radiant athletes at the start return home with gold medals at the end.

The result of the competition is not a parade of medalwinners, but, rather, as could be expected, a cross section of the totality of educational training. It is in addition a cross section from quite an early phase in the selection process, considering the large number of undergraduate students.

For students, training is not a simple process of acquiring knowledge and skills. It is a process of trial and error, of detours, stagnation, leaps forward and leaps into the dark. 'Maturity' is a problematic criterion when judging student plans, because anyone following a training course is by definition not yet mature in the profession he is being trained in. The learning period can better be regarded as a time of 'unripeness' and 'ripening', as the Polish writer Witold Gombrowicz puts it. What a jury may judge to be an 'immature' plan, may be an important step forward in the learning period. In Olympic terms: a new personal best.

As well as this, students sometimes want to go further than they are able, and pretend they already have the knowledge they are still busy acquiring. They are already rehearsing for their later role. In the competition entries this is evident in the eagerness with which the participants refer and quote. All ideas and references which are in vogue in the mature architectural debate can be found here, but then usually in half-understood and sometimes caricatural forms. The relation between the architectural design and the explanatory text is also often immature and laboured. Sometimes the text labours under grand gestures in time and space while the building designed looks modest or naive, and sometimes the design itself is a wild gesture which is not explained in the text. A recurring phenomenon is the over-literal translation of conceptual ideas in a design.

In addition, the texts make it abundantly clear that architecture and writing are two different professions. Only a handful of the commentaries are at all pleasant to read, such as a few Australian rehashings of old stories (Babel, the Big Bang) with the architecture school now occupying the lead role, and an essay on urban renewal in Beirut, which is a breath of fresh air just for its calm reasoning. Opposed to this there are numerous commentaries which rumble and creak and which make a somewhat desperate impression with all their capital letters and bold and italicised and underlined passages and triple dots...

The downside to all this trying so hard, is that the influence of personal experiences, doubts and lifestyles remains obscure. At best they can be deduced indirectly, and at the risk of all too banal psychologizing. In many entries the usefulness, the raison d'etre and the future of architecture, architectural training or even the world in general, is called

into doubt. For example, Christine Beveridge from Perth (Australia) takes the apocalypse as the point of departure for her design: human existence, and therefore the continued teaching of architecture, will from now on have to be done underground. In Andrew Lane's retelling of the story of the Tower of Babel, with the 'school of architecture' in the role of Babel, it ends just as badly as in the original version.[1] From Germany, two Irish students sent two joint entries. One is a photo of a tablet with the text: 'ArchitecTONIC. Take one tablet every 4-6 hours.' The other begins with: 'Architectural education is suffering from an identity crisis', a beguilingly ambiguous sentence.

The jury was angered by the 'negativity' expressed in these and other entries. But could the doubts expressed not be as much personal as professional? Does not every student have periodic attacks of doubt and love-hate feelings about his studies?

A 'personal vision' was asked for in the competition brief but it is not immediately clear which personal circumstances, experiential world, style and preferences such a vision arises from. There are few traces to be found in the entries of gangsta-rap, Kurt Cobain or a penchant for horseriding, although it is intriguing to encounter Maradona in a collage from China. There are numerous references to the ubiquitousness of the culture of images, but it is not clear whether these are signs of personal habits or fascination, or whether it just betrays obedience to the convention. At most one can detect, with some inventiveness, references to lifestyles, for example in the design by Diana Ramirez Jasso and three others from Guadalajara (Mexico) for a school which is suspended precariously above a ravine. At first glance that would seem to refer once again to the precariousness of architectural education, but nevertheless the atmosphere is different. It is the atmosphere of adventure and consumable danger, and if you want you can read into it references to the culture of skateboarding, MTV and Pepsi Max: 'Bungee Jump. An open encounter with the abyss. The will to embrace it, to surround

it. Elastic bands allowing us the impossible, the dream of flying, just as
Wenders' Kassiel. ... Architecture as the meeting point between how we wish
things were and how those things are made.'

The entries also offer an indirect glimpse of educational conditions. The use
of material varies from glossy A2 photos from Hong Kong and multi-media
collages from the US to cut-and-paste jobs from China and Iran, pencil
sketches on cheap paper, stuck onto cardboard. Two video tapes, two floppy
discs and from Zadar (Croatia) a baroque CD, were also submitted. Outside
the regions already mentioned, the PC is by no means common. The
correspondence about the competition showed that fax machines are quite
generally available, even though students from Nigeria had to visit a Shell
office to do it. Courier services are common in the rich countries especially.
In the light of digitization and globalization, Nwosu Obinna Elias, Jennifer
Wrobelski and Sammet Collins deserve special mention. Sent on 7 March
from Enugu (Nigeria), with the caveat: 'God knows when it will arrive',
Elias's registration reached the NAi on 24 April (it was not followed by an
entry). This 48-day journey made it the undisputed winner of the `longest
en route' category - that is, until 6 June when the entry by Wrobelski and
Collins arrived from Springfield (USA): sent on 15 April, it had been on its
way for 52 days.

Furthermore, it is nice to speculate about the teachers' approaches. The
seventeen entries from the Ural Academy of Architecture and Arts in
Jekaterinaburg are a striking illustration of this. Ten of the seventeen
students were supervised by the professors Elena Postnikova and Elena
Iovleva, and the seven entries by second year students in particular show
striking similarities. Here the competition brief seems to have been
combined with another task which could have been something like this:
make an expressive argument based on a single, simple metaphor. It
produced entries which explore future architectural education on the basis
of borscht, a caterpillar, the clothes button or Mendel's genetics applied to
peas. Even the drawing style is similar.

An intriguing question, finally, is whether the entries reveal anything
about the relation between education and the professional practice and
perspectives it is educating for. The group of entries from Beirut made it
possible to go deeper into this, as did the entry - in some aspects extreme -
from Kazakhstan.

Two courses in Beirut, the Lebanese American University (LAU) and the Académie Libanaise des Beaux-Arts (ALBA), set aside time for the competition task, resulting in 12 and 9 entries respectively.

The place of origin awakens curiosity. Beirut has suffered almost twenty years of civil war, destruction, segmentation and neglect. As the city slowly disintegrated, the population grew by 350,000, refugees from the countryside. In three years time, 1984-1987, as many illegal dwellings were built in shanty districts as had been legally built in the preceding thirty years. There is by now a reconstruction plan for the city centre, developed by one of the biggest bureaus in the Middle East, Dar-al-Handasah Consultants, including a boulevard seven metres wider than the Champs Elysee. In the shadow of this glamourous centre plan, there are numerous other tasks for architects and planners in this city of 1.5 million people, more than half the population of the Lebanon.

Is there anything of all this to be found in the 21 entries? The competition task was for a design for a school of architecture and not a reconstruction plan, but is the Beirut context noticeable in those designs?

The answer is no, twenty times over, with at best an occasional brief hesitation. In only one case is the answer positive.

All kinds of international trends can be found here too: travelling schools, global photocollages, the 'information explosion', the excelsior of an ideal learning process expressed in buildings surging upward, the staging of experiences of nature and autonomous objects which try to say, along with Rem Koolhaas: 'Fuck context'.

Fourteen designs make no or only brief reference, to the context. Many of

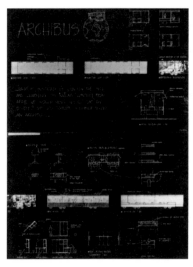

them are commented upon from the inside out, from educational wishes. 'A school of architecture should enable students to develop their own free thoughts', 'The ideal being an education that does not set the student on a definite path, but opens the possibilities for him to develop various "perspectives" of understanding', and 'My academy is reserved for a minority of people who have reached a certain level of culture', are a few typical statements. One of the two travelling schools, the bus by Sabine Moukheiber (ALBA), promises 'an environment worthy of career, worthy of the future.' About the context she writes simply: 'Context reflected in the glazing.' In a couple of cases the whole world is taken as context, and that also ultimately turns out to be vague and clumsy. For example, in 'One World' Rami

Khaled (LAU) develops his objective 'to unify students from different backgrounds' by connecting the separate building sections with footbridges. Two designs refer to the city only to exclude it. In one, this is done using a quote from Fumihiko Maki, much too heavy for this context, while the other, in the form of an eggtimer, consciously withdraws: 'Given the chaos of urban mushrooming, the future school of architecture reaches spirituality by means of abstraction.'

Four participants do place their school of architecture in an unmistakably urban context, even though in their explanation the urban culture exists more for the architectural students than the other way round. The city serves as decor for 'the perfect dynamic school', as 'A place for those who want to compete, challenge...And go on...' because: 'In the city we have all information within reach, and we have access to all sorts of new ideas in different fields (computer science, technical, urbanism...) and also access to construction sites.' Remarkably enough, the school by Marwan Sabeh Beaino (LAU) is located in Collins Street in Melbourne (Australia). But Paris, Beirut or Tokyo are also acceptable locations.

All four place their school in 'the' city, in a more or less interchangeable urban environment. In this, and in all twenty entries up to now, Beirut is at best present as an absence. The students' imagination flies far beyond the task of reconstruction at hand , into a world of haute architecture. Their immediate environment is the dream wish of cosmopolitanism. If the shattered city of Beirut has influenced the twenty entries, then it is perhaps in this indirect way. Beirut was once a sophisticated, cosmopolitan city. The entrants seem to want to skip the lengthy, laborious healing

process which now faces the city and to go on as if war and reconstruction have never happened.

With a single exception, a single entry in which architecture does not get its opportunity again after the healing but explicitly contributes to the reconstruction. 'Architecture: social condenser' by Nathalie Mahfoud (ALBA) is primarily a strategy for urban renewal, not for 'the' city, not for Beirut as a whole, but for specific spots in the decrepit neighbourhood of Achrafieh. Even this choice is for the

non-spectacular, because the neighbourhood apparently suffers not from dramatic bomb craters, but 'only' from neglect. It is precisely whilst being so specific, that the plan acquires universal significance: 'This issue exists in Lebanon as well as the rest of the world (the Bronx, Favellas...)'
Here the school of architecture gets a place 'in the least suspected place', and education is interwoven with the issues and potentials of the immediate surroundings. Almost nonchalantly, Mahfoud also provides the design for a school building. It is a simple, semi-permanent structure slid under a viaduct; a down-to-earth building far removed from the spectacular pieces of her fellow citizens and schoolmates.
Just as architecture for Mahfoud is a 'social condenser', some of the fine statements by other Lebanese entrants are absorbed by her plan. A school which teaches architects 'to care for the environment and to be preservers as well as creators (Lynn Bordcosh), in the midst of the dynamic city (Sandra Chacar, Wissam Doaboul), in 'a place where the existing is always questionable' (Elias Bechara Boustany): while in other entries these themes are only connected with difficulty to their elaboration, here they are in place. There are few entries which respond so precisely to the competition task which was to design a school of architecture 'from your own personal vision of the future role of architecure and architect'. This is not a school of architecture looking for a context or reasons to exist - the raison d'etre arises naturally from the urban problem, the context is waiting, the school is precisely what is needed.

Some plans, from the Netherlands for example, could be made ready for development tomorrow, so to speak. The sobriety of the impending professional practice seems to have already been absorbed, with the broad vista becoming a nuance. This is in sharp contrast to the entry by Constantin Moryak from North Kazakhstan, 'Architecture as a synthesis of human abilities and achievements in space and time'. He first describes the unstable situation in his country and then makes a giant leap towards an almost Platonic ideal of education:
'The challenge... lies in continuing economic, political and social instability, influencing the reform process.
This instability takes place also in the system of education (architectural as well). To deal with current problems of forming architectural environment in man's everyday life it is necessary to find more complex, qualitative, perfect solutions using the advanced engineering and scientific achievements.'

His school of architecure brings to mind simultaneously the production of top athletes in the former German Democratic Republic and the splendid Studio for experimental child architecture by Wladislaw Kirpitschow in Moscow: the most talented children will be selected at a young age and then carefully prepared for years, for their future task, 'according to laws of beauty and harmony'. Then comes the specialized architectural training, 'using up-to-date methods and technologies'. This text was written on an old-fashioned typewriter, 'which I didn't think existed any longer', remarked an amazed jury member. The enclosed drawing depicts the imagined educational process in a cosmic fantasy which includes an angel, a foetus, a galleon, and a spiral-shaped plinth for the sun. It is not the sort of presentation drawing which is immediately revealing to a client, but perhaps in the Kazakhstan context it is just realistic not to bear a client in mind.

This entry makes clear something which is implied in many others too: the design for the desired school of the future can also be read as a commentary on the school of the present and on the impending professional perspectives. The more the current situation is experienced as a swamp, the more beautiful paradise must be. At the same time the swamp of the present defines the possibilities of imagining a paradise.

The competition task asked students still in the midst of their training to transcend it and even to cast a visionary eye on the future. And much as they wanted to do it, the task was probably too difficult for practically everyone. 'It's like the Baron von Münchhausen who wanted to extract himself from the swamp', remarked one of the jury members. Perhaps the design task was as impossible as Münchhausen's achievement. But the reference to the Baron also shows that wrestling with the impossible can also lead to stories that are beautiful, even if - or just because - they are not completely convincing.

1 In Brisbane, Australia. Lane was probably not aware that the same tower had played an important - and more constructive - role in the Architecture & Education exhibition 'The making of the architect' in the NAi.

| * | HONOURABLE MENTION |
| ** | FIRST PRIZE |

USA, 66 ENTRIES, 21 SCHOOLS
Ann Arbor, University of Michigan
Manus Jirasetpatana	mnj5
Naazneen Jehan Rahman	nzsk
Mark Ayers	weez96
Arlington, University of Texas at Arlington
| Dan Gonzalez +1 | no.5 |
Blackburg, Virginia Polytechnic Institute and State University
| Robert Bristow +1 | ippirb |
Champaign, University of Illinois at Urbana-Champaign
| Hassan A. Gardezi | 3137 |
Denver, University of Colorado
James A. McWhorter	master
Stephen J. Baker +1	psmjtb
Robert D. Blount +2	djrbkl
Michael Lin +1	anmiwa
Detroit, University of Detroit Mercy
| Alan Alcid | ara200 |
Fayetteville, University of Arkansas
| Christy Hall-Merritt +1 | 1hm3 |
Houston, University of Houston
Cecilia Nguyen +1	colony
James Mol	jm6757
Franco Albarran	fa1344
Landon Parnell	lp1434
Mario Villena	mv4001
Mick Markham	mm5332
Ruth Duenes	rd4791
Michael Nolen	mn6132
Scott McCarthy	sm9957
Chuck Webb	cw6009
Lisa Matthews	lm6730
Hector Garcia +2	bbarch
Troy Douglas	td9587
Thanhtruc L. Hale	th1161
Ithaca, Cornell University / Harvard University
| Eric Höweler +1 | jmyeh2 |
Lexington, University of Kentucky
Lily Thuy Tien Le	gaea
Jennifer Wood	keel
Jeffery Pickett	spina
Zachary R. Wethington	diesel
Peter Priesler	aeolus
Jeffery Phelps	danza
Derek Guffey	summit
Mark Peter Meinhart	poeta
Curtis Thrush	fuzz23
Jennifer Lee Lewis	triade
Los Angeles, University of Southern California
| Neil Rubenstein | aabnrm |
| Roderico Ibanez | timide |

Matthew Baran	xbot715
Jay Jugueta Baliwag	jb4sc3
Niloofar Shokoohy	801lan
Miami, Florida International University
| Mauricio Del Valle | 3431 |
Milwaukee, University of Wisconsin
| Eric Mayne +1 | fsarup |
Missouri, Drury College
| Jennifer Wrobleski | gg8713 |
| Sammet Collins | dc123 |
New York, Columbia University
| Sheryl L. Kasak | k.o819. |
New York, Rensselaer Polytechnic Institute
| Lissa Parrott | lis789 |
Raleigh, North Carolina State University
Tom Langlois	tcl123
Philip D'Agostino	dagost
Evia Moseley	quoz35
James King	jfk348
Jamey Glueck	xx0077
Shawn Corbin	050274
Ian Gordon	127605
Derek Hopkins	96uca2
Kerry Finley	kgf126
David Sledge	456226
Jeffrey Schroeder	18062j
Philadelphia, Philadelphia College of Textiles & Science
| **Simon Koumjian 111 +4 | 171717 |
Princeton, Princeton University
| William Corwin | wcgs98 |
St Louis, Washington University
Susan Fox +1	dbgp
Joshua Nathaniel Mandell	diojec
Edward Saum +1	hmr2fl
Lisa Eun-Hwa Kim +1	archua
CFA
| James Saisakorn +1 | turnip |

NETHERLANDS, 55 ENTRIES, 11 SCHOOLS
Amsterdam, Academie van Bouwkunst
Sylvie Smeets +2	nriheg
Tom Baars +2	search
Lillian Brants +2	vulkan
Anniek Gehlen +1	inform
Rolf Bekker	tracks
Maurice Jennekens +1	ad2001
Han-Willem Visscher	engawa
Carli Driessen	ankers
A.T. Reedijk +2	70rh72
Amsterdam, Universiteit van Amsterdam
| Marie-Jose Zondag +1 | cabcar |
Arnhem, Technische Faculteit Hogeschool Gelderland
| de heer Caspara | caspara |
Delft, TU Delft

Court Haegens	what-is
Tom Bergevoet +1	255910
Paula Joao Carvalho Dias	tlzna
Floris van der Poel	021011
Dennis Kaspori	expere
*Evelyn v/d Ploeg +1	torens
David Ellens	transa
Saskia Simon	s-619
Markus Emmenegger	travel.2
Jan Kapsenberg	cubo35
M.J.P. Van Dooren	around
Pedro Marta	ltxhu
Rob Hendriks	sporen
Meta Berghauser Pontt +1	506019
Michiel Quirin Vrehen	bi-m

Eindhoven, TU Eindhoven

Wilbert de Haan +3	dna
Hans Ten Brinke +1	d!rive
Appie Hielkema	weimar
Brigit Van Bakel	991999
Jeroen Wouters	jwo496
Jan Van de Meulen +1	mdjm96

Rotterdam, Academie van Bouwkunst

Richard Breit	fa2003
5 T members +4	mas007

Rotterdam, Erasmus Universeit

Maaike Delemarre	moreys
Selma Kers	growth
Immo Nijhof	hubbab
Charlotte Wiering	klosh
M. Quist	quim52
Cecilia de Vries	quarts
Annemieke van Maanen	maan
Astrid de Haas	241273
D.G.M. Commandeur	diy21
Mirielle v.d. Steen	steen
Natalie Cornelissen	paddos
Daniella Pijnen	alfa96
Rick Dolphijn	downup
	around
Mark van Westerlaak	water

Tilburg, Academie van Bouwkunst

Peter Van Gisbergen	ae4p&f

Tilburg, Hogeschool Midden-Brabant

Ruud van der Koelen	br1
Alexander Van Straten +1 juego	

Utrecht, Hogeschool van Utrecht

Rutger Pasman	asrp4u
Bart Melk +2	p=3.14m

Wageningen, Landbouw Universiteit

Anko Grootveld +4	cofa 04

ITALY, 29 ENTRIES, 10 SCHOOLS

Chieti, Universita degli studi 'G. d'Annunzio'

Andrea Petrecca	ucb
Simone Barlafante +4	pe96p4
Simone Barlafante +4	pe96p3
Simone Barlafante +4	pe96p2
Simone Barlafante +4	pe96p1

Firenze, Universita Degli Studi Di Firenze

Leonardo Bianchi	12ld29
Bicci Eugenio +2	cbalop

Genoa, Universita degli studi di Genova

Pulselli Gabriele +3	pemp
Lorena Mario +1	malo

Lentini, Universita degli Studi di Reggio Calabria

Fabio Zagami +1	zaelid

Milan, Politecnico di Milano

Lorenzo Lotesto	ab805
Claudia Della Torre	tavola
Antonio Maria Tedeschi +6	unid96

Palermo, Università degli studi di Palermo

Renato Ceraulo +2	rc2t73
Marchisciana Adriano	060372
Maria Maida	fr23lo

Rome, Terza Università Statale degli studi di Roma

Marco Sambo	artre

Rome, Universita degli Studi di Roma La Sapienza

Silvia Federici	sf01lr
Fabio Tudisco +1	palm30
Luca Falchi	docere

Turin, Politecnico di Torino, Facolta di Architettura

Cesare Griffa	unvrsl
Andrea Veglia +1	aufs01
Ivan Bianco +1	bb1701
Giuseppe Guerico	aganor
Federico Villa +2	carica
Francesca Steffenoni +1	avf501

Venice, Istituto Universitario di Architettura di Venezia

Mario Bagna +1	me1970
Erika Calligaro	ivav.
Stefano Mondini +1	scbf01

RUSSIA, 27 ENTRIES, 4 SCHOOLS

Krasnoyarsk, State Academy of Architecture and Civil Engineering

Julia Rachmatyllina	123457
Nataly Krasnoperov	nvka29
Nataly Sviridova	197522
Stanislav Baranov	660000
Vadim Shmal	051320
Anton Ansov	777666
Voldemar Axochakov	541974

Samara, Academy of Architecture and Construction

Matvey Malakhov	jumbo
Natalia Mikhailova	a2992
Ekaterina Kirillova	250374

Volgograd, State Academy of Architacture and Civil Engineering

Anton Tolochko	223606

Yekaterinburg, Ural Academy of Architecture & Arts

Vladislav Spitsyn +1	7re555
Boudantseva Tatiana	levels
Ilya Ponomaryev +1	6000df
Nathalia Shibaeva +1	150276

Kaganovich Alexi	sand77
Vladimir Gromada	950570
Marat Ibragimov	654321
Irina Makarova	461780
Anna Ansimova	357544
Marina Shiganova	4marn2
Ivan Zanchevskiy	ar3432
Nastia Miroshnikova	313156
*Svetlana Nekrasova	160196
Irina Konoshencko	734521
Polina Taranenko	90677a
Ardeeva Svetlana	07274
Eugene Zhvirblite	e1876g

AUSTRALIA, 25 ENTRIES, 5 SCHOOLS
Adelaide, University of Adelaide

Alex Munt +1	manti5
Nick Brand +1	enigma
John Bralic	eep107
Julian Worrall	truc07

Brisbane, University of Queensland

Christopher David Lee	lee123
Peter Besley	palace
Jim Lau	ecotopia
Jamie Peel	making
Angus Munro +2	2233am

Melbourne

John Bornas +3	tadj-4

Melbourne

Andrew Lane	babel

Perth, Curtin University of Technology

Natalie Andrea Edwards	idy3
Joanna Louise Gibson	tonic
Tuan Anh Duong +1	stadtt
Jemma Carlee Williams	940914
Natalie O'Hart	94572a
Dana Sims	31849b
*Christine Beveridge	954184
Sarah Jane Beeck +2	blm524
Amzah Zainal	point2
Penelope Forlano	912169d
Gaye Elizabeth McKean	3439gm
Leonie Cownie	30415j
Wei-Jen Henry Lin	hd168

University of New South Wales

Ben Hewett +2	bhamab

UNITED KINGDOM, 25 ENTRIES, 13 SCHOOLS
Aberdeen, Robert Gordon University

20 students	no motto

Edinburgh, Edinburgh University

Patrick Ground	ground

Glasgow, Mackintosh School of Architecture

Jose Manuel Garcia +1	179320

Hull, University of Humberside

Hairul Nizar Tamaddun	zr7073

Leeds, Leeds Metropolitan University

Nigel Pilkington	drnp

Leicester, De Montfort University

Steve Gittner +1	gitcar
Howard Jones +1	0078
Mark Limbrick +2	live-in
Olaf Herzog	3720

London, London Guildhall University

Pedro Sepulveda Sandoval	pass69

Londen, South Bank University

Leonidas Pantazopoulos	4532
Electra Mikelides	rup96
Joyce Ko-Hsin Chan	jc1112

London, Architectural Association School of Architecture

*Kate Darby +1	g24k31
Aaron Chetwynd +1	1daful
Hiroki Ishikawa	hi518
Koichi Takada	k2

London, Bartlett School of Arch. & Planning

*Christina Diaz-Moreno	9nueve

London, University of East London

*Yahya Al-Tahin Aliraqi +1	mus 965
Christopher Romanos +1	otcr1
Mark Tuff +1	poppy
Katja Hasche +1	29041612

Nottingham, University of Nottingham

Irina Davidovici	9887id

Sheffield, University of Sheffield

Loizos Antonios Fantis	2k3mad

Newcastle-upon-Tyne, University of Newcastle-upon-Tyne

Nick Readett-Bayley	nick44

LEBANON, 21 ENTRIES, 2 SCHOOLS
Beirut, Académie Libanaise des Beaux-Arts

Elias Bechara Boustany	ebl333
Joumana Ferzli	jf1673
Nada Talhame	nad666
Rania Sassine	rs1021
Sabine Moukheiber	bs2904
Aline Asmar	ab0392
Marwan Sabeh Beaino	mb0572
Nathalie Mahfoud	270673
Sandra Chacar	240274

Byblos, Lebanese American University

Lara Bechwaty	l1129b
Maya Zoghaib	mz9900
Lynn Bordcosh	jlb730
Remy Costantine	rm7413
Wissam Doaboul	nr3321
Nadim Maalouf +1	nm96mk
Rami Khaled	rk839k
Khoury Andre	al111k
Ali Wazani	aw4uhh
Richard Abi-Habib	rah135
Antoine Boulos	tb446a
Wissam Assaker	wa7113

BELGIUM,18 ENTRIES, 6 SCHOOLS
Brussel, Hogeschool v Wetenschap en Kunst
Filip Smits +1   935ice
Brussel, Vrije Universiteit Brussel
Sven Hebbelinck   spacex
Jan Cuypers +1   meduca
Stouffs Inge   dim
Alick Gerené   plugin
Troost Olivier   astoryy
Olivier Troost   astory
Tom Moons   wereld
Bart Verhasselt   hazel
Diepenbeek, Provinciaal Hoger Architectuurinstituut
Geert De Neuter +1   ca5
Gent, Hogeschool v Wetenschap en Kunst
Ewout Vandeweghe +1   noasis
Gent, Universiteit Gent
Philippe De Clerck   1985
Tournai Ecole de St. Luc
Vincent Ermel +1   26464
Yaun Gary +1   71174
Olivier Camus +4   52316
Isabelle Anceaux +1   11476
Delphine Derville +2   11007

CHINA , 16 ENTRIES, 4 SCHOOLS
Bei Jing, Institute of Civil Engineering & Architecture
Dong-yong Ren +1   ry
He Wang   hewang
Zhi-qi Li +1   hl5130
Xiao-lu Zhou Lay Jin +1   jz6822
Bei Jing, Hu Bei WuHan University - School of
Economics
Wu Yang   uterus
Bei Jing, WuHan University of Hydraulics & Electrical
Engineering
Chao Cheng & Shan yang   ys765
Mong Tong   fool
Kun Hu Xing Wang +1   460912
Bei Jing, WuHan University of Technology
N. Zhang   temple
Lisa   travel.1
Jinwei Zhang   jwzang
Li Mei   limei
Jilin, Jilin Institute of Architecture and Civil
Engineering
Wu Yingchun   731212
Li Keyan +1   750107
Jinan, Shandong Institute of Architecture &
Engineering
Qinghua Chai   no motto
Ting Liu   no motto

GERMANY, 16 ENTRIES, 11 SCHOOLS
Berlin, Technische Universität
Marc Richter   200960
Bremen, Hochschule Bremen
Manuela Böske   190762

Cologne, Fachhochschule Koln
Christin Ursprung   e12373
Oliver Kußeler   008150
Hannover, Universität Hannover
Dagmar Reinhardt   vert05
Theo Lorenz   234353
Munich, Fachhochschule München
Attila Baksa-So's   buda96
Munich, Technische Universität München
Bettina Gerhold +1   230596
? , Fachhochschule Rheinland-Pfalz
Holger Schnädelbach   05092h
Stuttgart, Staatliche Akademie der Bildenden Künste
Sigrid Schönenberger   sc3103
Stuttgart, Universität Stuttgart
Snadra Kötzle   770618
Hasan Dolan   10165h
Maren Harnack   ligeti
Weimar, Hochschule fur Architektur und Bauwesen
Weimar
Thorsten Schalk   3b7c9r
Aachen, RWTH Aachen / AvB Rotterdam
Claudia Schmidt +1   less4u

CANADA, 9 ENTRIES, 7 SCHOOLS
Montreal, McGill University
Mana Hemami   x10f13
Olivier Ottevaere +1   so7777
Ontario, University of Waterloo
Adriana Mot +1   mr2123
Quebec, Université Laval
Nathalie Chiasson +1   vene95
Toronto, Ontario College of Art
Athina Gatos +1   10d386
Toronto, University of Toronto
James Pitropov   xt7
Winnipeg, University of Manitoba
Vaike Ruus +1   chev51
Darren Burns   no motto
Winnipeg, Carleton University
Francesco Di Sarra   tagger

GUATEMALA, 9 ENTRIES, 2 SCHOOLS
Guatemala, Universidad Francisco Marroquin
Luis J. Saenz Morales   sagua1
Luisa María Dougherty De Wer   +110975
Williams M. Toledo Aquino   tole96
Shannon Drake Cruz   comm+11
Guatemala, Universidad Rafael Landivar
Sarah V.S. Ruiz   v54rt1
Lilly Acevedo Rivera   liooia
Jose O.Z. Descamps   jodj+1d
Cesar M.A.S. Orellana   khasco
Alberto S. Mendoza   a4s1+16

HONG KONG, 9 ENTRIES, 1 SCHOOL
Hong Kong, University of Hong Kong
Ivy Chan Kai Chu +1   chasiu

Marco Chan Pan Hang +1	maredd
Benny Ng Kit Wah +1	kkkkkk
Jim Ngai Yee Hong +1	shitan
*Oleum Chan Yung +1	kaukei
Kim-chung Cheung +1	ckclph
Margaret Chan Ting-Chee	mckm96
Emilie Hui Sau-Ling +1	nuisun
Wayne Mak Kiu-yan +1	kymch2

JAPAN, 9 ENTRIES, 4 SCHOOLS
Kobe, Kobe University
Kazumi Kudo +2	132426
Kyoto, Kyoto Institute of Technology
Ken-ichi Oka	172839
Wakako Mori	147147
Kimihide Okamoto	110748
Masanori Minami	00001
Masaaki Ogawa	1014
Akihiko Kunimoto	102256
Tiba, Tiba Institute of Technology
Endo Atsushi +1	2171
Tokyo, Science University of Tokyo
Hiroshi Iseya	isekan

BRAZIL, 8 ENTRIES, 8 SCHOOLS
Espirito Santo, Univ. Federal do Espirito Santo
Aidacileia Carminatti Lube +5	ufes17
Pelotas, Universidade Catolica de Pelotas
Laura Azevedo +2	docas3
Rio De Janeiro, Universidade Santa Ursula
Hueider Carvalho Cruz +1	bil171
Rodovia, Pontifícia Universidade Católica de Campinas
Adriano Carneval Domingues +1	simple
Sao Paulo, Faculdade de Belas Artes de Sao Paulo
Leandro Alegria Pereira +2	lsr477
Sao Paulo, Universidade Catolica De Santos
Luiz Renato Soares Leal +2	faus
Sao Paulo, Universidade de Sao Paulo
Brutus Abel Fratuce Pimentel +8	u-terere
Sao Paulo, Fundação Armando Alvares Penteado
Efsthathia Jean Vourakis +1	fauspo

MEXICO, 6 ENTRIES, 6 SCHOOLS
Chihuahua, Escuela de Arquitectura de Chihuahua
Raul Maldonado Anchondo +1	7a58cx
Guadalajara, ITESO - Instituto Tecnologico
Diana Ramirez Jasso	eolo04
Mexico
Albamar Hernandez +3	abva
Guadalajara, UNAM - Universidad
Lorenzo Rocha Cito	loi-107
Guadalajara, Universidad de Guanajuato
Alejandro Guzman Ramirez	kos73
Guadalajara, Universidad La Salle
Elizabeth Casillas +1	xdfo96

UKRAINE, 7 ENTRIES, 2 SCHOOLS
Dnepropetrovsk, State Academy of Civil Engineering
and Architecture
Rodion Tovstik	681060
Grigory Kramarov	806562
Maxim Vitalievich Lukyanov	703985
Jana Zakharova +1	979797
Elena Smirnova	311277
Lviv, L'vivska Polytechnyka State University
Yevgen Voronits +3	delmac
Stolyarov Juri	040774

POLAND, 7 ENTRIES, 4 SCHOOLS
Gdansk, Technical University of Gdansk
Kamil Tumelis +1	solus8
Anna Awtuch	xx01
Gliwice, Wydzial Architektury Politechniki Slaskiej
Przemyslaw Godycki +3	2xa273
Poznan, Poznan Techical University
Wojciech Przywecki	echinu
Szczecin	Polithnika
Szczecinska
Piotr Karabin	pk3004
Krzysztof Grzegorzewski +1	541868
Poznan, Silesian Technical University
Lukasz Zagala +1	997000

DENMARK, 6 ENTRIES, 2 SCHOOLS
Copenhagen, Danmarks Designskole - Institute of Spatial Design
Kim Norland	tower9990
Sofia Hedkvist	karibu
Copenhagen, Denmark's International Study Programme
Seung Chul Paek	091971
David Wang	032570
Domenico Francesco Lio	123456
Copenhagen, University of Copenhagen
James Haeseker	112371

FRANCE, 6 ENTRIES, 5 SCHOOLS
Darnétal, Ecole d'Architecture de Normandie
Jean-Luc Boulard	hou123
Nanterre, Ecole d'Architecture de Paris la Défense
Asja Bajbutovic	jazzz
Paris, Ecole d'Architecture de Paris La Villette
Yvan Ikhlef	eos+141
Marijke Troost	abcxyz
Paris, L'Ecole d'Architecture de Paris la Seine
Chang Ji-Hoon	semo96
Paris, Ecole d'Architecture de Paris Belleville
Saskia Kloosterboer	ne&sk

CROATIA, 4 ENTRIES, 1 SCHOOL
Zagreb, University of Zagreb
Davor Silov	davor/55553
Vedran Duplancic +1	sun021023
Damir Ljutie	vlayo1
Vedran Pedisic +1	kb41.8

KAZAKHSTAN, 4 ENTRIES, 2 SCHOOLS
Akmola, Akmola Agricultural Institute
Konstantin Moryak   529348
Tselinograd, Tselinograd Agricultural Institute
Vasily Prilipuchin   vas666
Dimitry Linenko   ldv211
Evgeny Svetlichny   seo111

TURKEY, 4 ENTRIES, 2 SCHOOLS
Ankara, Middle East Technical University
Vehbi Inan   753939
Faith Erduman   572366
Istanbul, Istanbul Technical University
Seda Kula +1   orion
Irem Mollaahmetoglu   888

FINLAND, 3 ENTRIES, 2 SCHOOLS
Helsinki, Helsinki University of Technology
Päivi Kiuru Kiuru +2   px3o1a
Oulu, University of Oulu
Antti Lassila +1   phaze3
Oiva Vesa +1   scion

IRAN, 3 ENTRIES, 1 SCHOOL
Tehran, Shahid Beheshti University
Taghi Taghisadeh   taghi
Hootan Ahmadi Hamedani   sh5563
Sanaz Eftekhar Zadeh   455547

SPAIN, 3 ENTRIES, 2 SCHOOLS
Madrid, Universidad Politécnica de Madrid
Oscar Rodriguez Fernandez   005car
Angel Sevillano Martin   aa239f
Madrid, Universite Complutense de Madrid
*Guillaume De Malet Roquefort   xxxII

THAILAND, 3 ENTRIES, 3 SCHOOLS
Bangkok, Rajamangala Institute of Technology
Puttichart Wanichtat +1   put010
Bangkok, Chulalongkorn University / Silpakorn
University
Sunthorn & Busadee   no motto 5
Khon Kaen   Khon Kaen
University
Pojchara Jatupoj   no motto 2

INDIA, 2 ENTRIES, 1 SCHOOL
Ahmedabad, Ahmedabad School of Architecture
Meghal Jain +1   208144
Gertjan Nijhoff +1   220296

INDONESIA, 2 ENTRIES, 1 SCHOOL
Bandung,Parahyangan Catholic University
Anindhita N. Sunartio +2   kaja14
Andre Kusprianto   a9149

IRELAND, 2 ENTRIES, 1 SCHOOL
Jonathan Bennett +1   l1418j

Liam Brennan +1   732b72

CZECH REP, 2 ENTRIES, 1 SCHOOL
Prague, Czech Technical University of Prague
Osamu Okamura   pogch
Katerina Konecna   538144

NIGERIA, 2 ENTRIES, 1 SCHOOL
Lagos, University of Lagos
Leslie Ohomele   le2312
David Irvoje Aigbodion   ram318

SWITZERLAND, 2 ENTRIES, 2 SCHOOLS
Geneva, Ecole d'Ingénieurs de Genève
Dirk Schmid +1   brains
Zurich   ETH Zurich
Andri Gerber +1   lexi

AUSTRIA, 1 ENTRY, 1 SCHOOL
Wien, Technische Universität Wien
Wolfgang Koelbl   3xi505

ESTONIA, 1 ENTRY, 1 SCHOOL
Tallinn, Tallinn Art University
Siiri Vallner +1   vst001

GEORGIA,1 ENTRY, 1 SCHOOL
Tbilisi, Georgian Polytechnical Institute
Murtaz Beraia   129789

GHANA, 1 ENTRY, 1 SCHOOL
Kumasi, University of Science and Technology
Daniel Ashai Adashie   danash

ISRAEL, 1 ENTRY, 1 SCHOOL
Jerusalem, Bezalel Academy of Arts
Stefan Davidovich   prg805

LITHUANIA, 1 ENTRY, 1 SCHOOL
Vilnius, Vilnius, Technical University
Tomas Lape +1   f22723

PORTUGAL, 1 ENTRY, 1 SCHOOL
Porto, Universidade do Porto
Fernando de Castro Goncalves +2 f3pp57

SERBIA, 1 ENTRY, 1 SCHOOL
Belgrade, Belgrade Faculty of Architecture
Aleksandar Ignjatovic +2   yay

VENEZUELA, 1 ENTRY, 1 SCHOOL
Caracas, Universidad Caracas Venezuela
Jose Mora +2   ccsmwc

                                 fossilis
                                 3i4r5o

Illustrations

Design: Joseph Plateau, graphic designers, Amsterdam
Reproduction Photography: Martien Kerkhof, Studio Retina, Amsterdam
Translation text Fred Feddes: Michael O'Loughlin
Translation text Arthur Wortmann: Jane Zuyl-Moores
Printing: Waanders, Zwolle
Production: Marianne Lahr
Publisher: Simon Franke

The programme Architecture and Education was made possible by the
Dutch Fund for Architecture, Rotterdam.

This publication was made possible by the Ministry of Education, Culture
and Science.

Printed and Bound in the Netherlands
Available in North, South and Central America through
D.A.P./Distributed Art Publishers 636 Broadway, 12th floor,
New York, NY 10012, Tel. 212 473-5119 Fax 212 673-2887

ISBN 90-5662-032-0

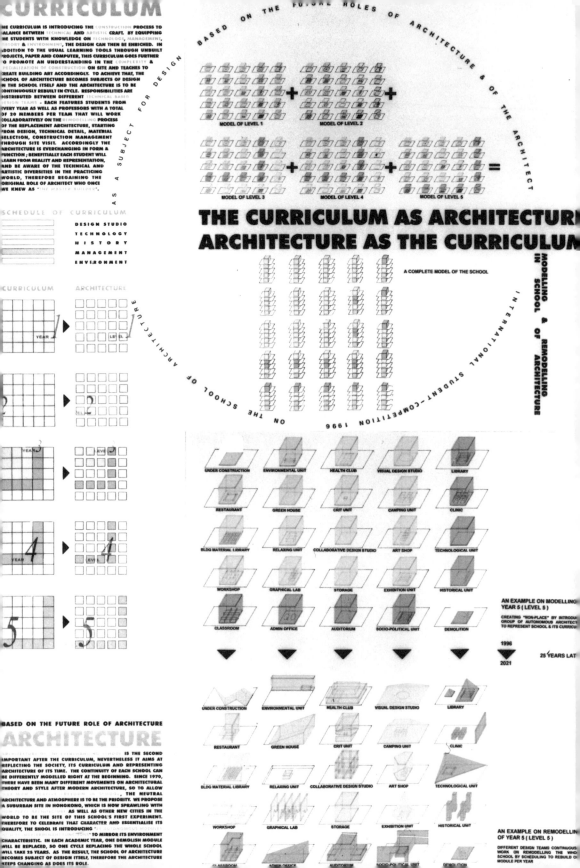

CURRICULUM

THE CURRICULUM IS INTRODUCING THE CONSTRUCTION PROCESS TO BALANCE BETWEEN TECHNICAL AND ARTISTIC CRAFT. BY EQUIPPING THE STUDENTS WITH KNOWLEDGE ON TECHNOLOGY, MANAGEMENT, HISTORY & ENVIRONMENT, THE DESIGN CAN THEN BE ENRICHED. IN ADDITION TO THE USUAL LEARNING TOOLS THROUGH UNBUILT PROJECTS, PAPER AND COMPUTER, THIS CURRICULUM GOES FURTHER TO PROMOTE AN UNDERSTANDING IN THE COMPLEXITY & SPECIALIZATION OF CONSTRUCTION ON SITE AND TEACHES TO CREATE BUILDING ART ACCORDINGLY. TO ACHIEVE THAT, THE SCHOOL OF ARCHITECTURE BECOMES SUBJECTS OF DESIGN IN THE SCHOOL ITSELF AND THE ARCHITECTURE IS TO BE CONTINUOUSLY REBUILT IN CYCLE. RESPONSIBILITIES ARE DISTRIBUTED BETWEEN DIFFERENT TECHNICAL BASED DESIGN TEAMS. EACH FEATURES STUDENTS FROM EVERY YEAR AS WELL AS PROFESSORS WITH A TOTAL OF 20 MEMBERS PER TEAM THAT WILL WORK COLLABORATIVELY ON THE REMODELLING PROCESS OF THE REPLACEMENT ARCHITECTURE, STARTING FROM DESIGN, TECHNICAL DETAIL, MATERIAL SELECTION, CONSTRUCTION MANAGEMENT THROUGH SITE VISIT. ACCORDINGLY THE ARCHITECTURE IS EVERCHANGING IN FORM & FUNCTION ; BENEFITIALLY EACH STUDENT WILL LEARN FROM REALITY AND REPRESENTATION, AND BE AWARE OF THE TECHNICAL AND ARTISTIC DIVERSITIES IN THE PRACTICING WORLD, THEREFORE REGAINING THE ORIGINAL ROLE OF ARCHITECT WHO ONCE WE KNEW AS "THE MASTER BUILDER".

AS A SUBJECT FOR DESIGN

BASED ON THE FUTURE ROLES OF ARCHITECTURE & OF THE ARCHITECT

MODEL OF LEVEL 1 + MODEL OF LEVEL 2 +

MODEL OF LEVEL 3 + MODEL OF LEVEL 4 + MODEL OF LEVEL 5 =

THE CURRICULUM AS ARCHITECTURE
ARCHITECTURE AS THE CURRICULUM

A COMPLETE MODEL OF THE SCHOOL

MODELLING IN SCHOOL & REMODELLING OF ARCHITECTURE

INTERNATIONAL STUDENT-COMPETITION 1996
ON THE SCHOOL OF ARCHITECTURE

SCHEDULE OF CURRICULUM

DESIGN STUDIO
TECHNOLOGY
HISTORY
MANAGEMENT
ENVIRONMENT

CURRICULUM   ARCHITECTURE

YEAR   LEVEL

UNDER CONSTRUCTION | ENVIRONMENTAL UNIT | HEALTH CLUB | VISUAL DESIGN STUDIO | LIBRARY
RESTAURANT | GREEN HOUSE | CRIT UNIT | CAMPING UNIT | CLINIC
BLDG MATERIAL LIBRARY | RELAXING UNIT | COLLABORATIVE DESIGN STUDIO | ART SHOP | TECHNOLOGICAL UNIT
WORKSHOP | GRAPHICAL LAB | STORAGE | EXHIBITION UNIT | HISTORICAL UNIT
CLASSROOM | ADMIN OFFICE | AUDITORIUM | SOCIO-POLITICAL UNIT | DEMOLITION

AN EXAMPLE ON MODELLING
YEAR 5 (LEVEL 5)

CREATING "NON-PLACE" BY INTRODUCING GROUP OF AUTONOMOUS ARCHITECTS TO REPRESENT SCHOOL & ITS CURRICULUM

1996
2021
25 YEARS LATER

UNDER CONSTRUCTION | ENVIRONMENTAL UNIT | HEALTH CLUB | VISUAL DESIGN STUDIO | LIBRARY
RESTAURANT | GREEN HOUSE | CRIT UNIT | CAMPING UNIT | CLINIC
BLDG MATERIAL LIBRARY | RELAXING UNIT | COLLABORATIVE DESIGN STUDIO | ART SHOP | TECHNOLOGICAL UNIT
WORKSHOP | GRAPHICAL LAB | STORAGE | EXHIBITION UNIT | HISTORICAL UNIT
CLASSROOM | ADMIN OFFICE | AUDITORIUM | SOCIO-POLITICAL UNIT | DEMOLITION

AN EXAMPLE ON REMODELLING
OF YEAR 5 (LEVEL 5)

DIFFERENT DESIGN TEAMS CONTINUOUSLY WORK ON REMODELLING THE WHOLE SCHOOL BY SCHEDULING TO REBUILD ONE MODULE PER YEAR

BASED ON THE FUTURE ROLE OF ARCHITECTURE
ARCHITECTURE

ARCHITECTURE OF THE MATERIAL WORLD IS THE SECOND IMPORTANT AFTER THE CURRICULUM, NEVERTHELESS IT AIMS AT REFLECTING THE SOCIETY, ITS CURRICULUM AND REPRESENTING ARCHITECTURE OF ITS TIME. THE CONTINUITY OF EACH SCHOOL CAN BE DIFFERENTLY MODELLED RIGHT AT THE BEGINNING. SINCE 1970, THERE HAVE BEEN MANY DIFFERENT MOVEMENTS ON ARCHITECTURAL THEORY AND STYLE AFTER MODERN ARCHITECTURE, SO TO ALLOW THE ARCHITECTURE REPRESENTATION, THE NEUTRAL ARCHITECTURE AND ATMOSPHERE IS TO BE THE PRIORITY. WE PROPOSE A SUBURBAN SITE IN HONGKONG, WHICH IS NOW SPRAWLING WITH WORLD TO BE THE SITE OF THIS SCHOOL'S FIRST EXPERIMENT. THEREFORE TO CELEBRATE THAT CHARACTER AND ESSENTIALISE ITS QUALITY, THE SHOOL IS INTRODUCING UNCONSCIOUS MODEL TO MIRROR ITS ENVIRONMENT CHARACTERISTIC. IN EACH ACADEMIC YEAR, ONE DEMOLISH MODULE WILL BE REPLACED, SO ONE CYCLE REPLACING THE WHOLE SCHOOL WILL TAKE 25 YEARS. AS THE RESULT, THE SCHOOL OF ARCHITECTURE BECOMES SUBJECT OF DESIGN ITSELF, THEREFORE THE ARCHITECTURE KEEPS CHANGING AS DOES ITS ROLE.